The   unty

"A truly incredible story! A testament to the human spirit that clearly illustrates how people from two entirely different social/economic backgrounds can come together and create something unique, even behind the walls of a state prison."

—*Ralph Johnson of Earth, Wind & Fire*

"Jay Warner's succinct and sparkling style brings the Prisonaires' story to life and proves among other things that, if you have talent, it shows through even from prison."

—*Ben Weisman, writer of fifty-seven songs for
Elvis Presley*

"Jay Warner's *Just Walkin' in the Rain,* the true story of Johnny Bragg and the Prisonaires, is a brilliant read about Afro-Americans who dared to dream at a time when, for Blacks, it was an 'Impossible Dream.'"

—*Mary Wilson of the Supremes*

"After 44 years in the music business, I thought I'd heard every great story there was and met every act worth knowing. This mesmerizing book proved to me that there was at least one more really worth knowing about. A true story that reads like a hit movie."

—*Ron Isley of the Isley Brothers*

"*Just Walkin' in the Rain* is a story of unbelievable love for music and how it can work wonders. No story can ever top the sad story of all that the Prisonaires went through—the hardship, pain, and glory. So, Jay, thanks for a true story that can bring you to tears and help you remember someone who truly paid their dues."

—*Ben E. King, legendary lead singer
of the Drifters*

"Awesome! *Just Walkin' in the Rain* is just awesome. The story of the Prisonaires made me want to cry for the troubled lives of the guys in the group and then cheer for their success. Johnny Bragg is a man who freed himself spiritually and triumphed over adversity to become a legend, and a hero 'in my book.' I could certainly relate to a lot of the hardship that the group experienced. And Governor Clement's positive spirit of justice is a commentary on the goodness inherent in us all."

—*Bubba Knight of Gladys Knight and the Pips*

"When the Jordanaires recorded with Johnny Bragg during the '50s, we really did not realize how amazing and contradictory his life was. I feel if it wasn't for Jay Warner's in-depth writings we and, I dare say, the general public would never know about this one-of-a-kind singer and songwriter and his incredible, chameleon-like story."

—*Gordon Stoker of the Jordanaires*

"Reading about the Prisonaires was an upsetting but very compelling experience. It's a great story and I'm glad that Jay Warner decided to write about these forgotten people."

—*Carl Gardner, founder and lead singer*
of the Coasters

"This book is very powerful, moving, and enlightening. I recommend it to people in and out of the music business. It's fascinating and will definitely grab your attention! Great job, Jay!"

—*Carvin Winans, leader of the Grammy-*
winning group the Winans

"One of the most entertaining books on the market today. I thought I knew all about vocal groups, but this one lets you know you can always learn something new."

—*Otis Williams of the Temptations*

Just Walkin' in the Rain

Just Walkin' in the Rain

Jay Warner

RENAISSANCE BOOKS
Los Angeles

Library of Congress Catalog Card Number: 00-108762
ISBN: 1-58063-140-1

Design by Jesús Arellano

Published by Renaissance Books
Distributed by St. Martin's Press
Manufactured in the United States of America
First edition

To my biggest believers: my mother, Ray Lillian Wax, my father, Robert Wayne Warner, my Uncle Archie "Willie" Friedberg, my Aunt Sydelle and Uncle Hymie Sherman, Sam Shatzman and my wife, Jackie. May your spirit, faith, and love forever guide me and may God always bless you.

Contents

Acknowledgments

First and foremost I'd like to thank Johnny Bragg for his painstaking recollections and contributions to this book. Also my thanks to Don Hildebrand for his steady steering of the Bragg ship and his insightful thoughts. And a special thanks to that Sherlock Holmes of the South, Mr. Dobie Gray (not many recording stars would run around Nashville doing research for a friend's book in the middle of recording an album).

My deep appreciation to the Clement family, particularly Congressman Bob Clement, Senator Anna Belle Clement O'Brien, and Judge Frank Clement Jr., for their time and reminiscences. Likewise, my sincere appreciation to Warden James "Droopy" Edwards for his concise stories and anecdotes.

I'd also like to thank the following people for their help: Rob Pooley (my invaluable assistant), Ben Weisman, John Wilson, Gordon Skadberg, Andy McKaie, George Moonagian, Peter Grendysa, Bill Millar, Victor Pearlin, Peter Guralnick, Colin Escott, Galen Gart, Misti Bragg, Mary Smith, Tom Kittrell, Ron Tropp, Jack Gunter, Eddie Jones, Jerry Shilling, Michael Dougherty, Dave Weiner, Larry Brinton, Bill Goodman, Ken Fieth (Metro Archives, Nashville), Ann M. Locke, Bjorn Jentoft, Dave Sanjek, Gordon Stoker, Joe Isgro, Gabe Tucker, Hank Davis, Lisa Lenthall, Jim Cole, Herschel Watson, Dan Malvin, Keith Albert (*Cash Box* magazine), John Koenig (*Discoveries* magazine), Greg Loesher (*Goldmine* magazine), Christie Rae, George Lavatelli, Maxine Hanson, Karla Buhlman, Kaylyn Keane, John Dougan (Memphis-Shelby County Archives), Karina McDaniels (Tennessee State Library and Archives), Cassie Hassler

(Tennessee State Library and Archives), Vince McGrath (Tennessee State Legislature).

I'd also like to thank Richard Weize (Bear Family Records); Carolyn Waugh; John Broven; Dave Booth; Mark Medley (Country Music Hall of Fame); Chris Guze (Country Music Association); Dennis Wolfe; Sam, Dorothy, and Cinnamon Atchley; Jerry Osbourne; and Marv Goldberg.

Moreover, my grateful appreciation to the staff at Renaissance, for your belief in this story and my presentation of it.

Lastly to my wife, Jackie, truly my in-house editor, who has tirelessly corrected my 2:00 A.M. typos and patiently encouraged me to finish what I start. I love you and I promise, *this time*, some time off in Europe before I start anything of this magnitude again.

Foreword by Rick Dees

I've been a fan and student of rock'n'roll since I was a kid playing air guitar with my buddies back in Greensboro, North Carolina. Since then, I've traversed the earth conducting archeological digs on the sites of ancient music stores and even descended to the bowels of musty basements in search of musical treasures to share with my listeners on the *Weekly Top 40 Countdown* and the *Rick Dees in the Morning* show. Thus it was with great appreciation and admiration that I discovered *Just Walkin' in the Rain,* the latest tome from fellow music archeologist Jay Warner.

Following up his acclaimed anthology of rock'n'roll, *Billboard's American Rock'n'Roll in Review,* Jay has unearthed and reconstructed a fantastic story of courage, heartbreak, hope, and redemption. At the epicenter of this story is Johnny Bragg, a little-known music legend and hero who overcame insurmountable odds to turn an odyssey of tragedy into a triumph of the human spirit.

Much more than a story of one man's journey to hell and back, this story is a poignant reminder of the social hardships and prejudices that ravaged much of America in the twentieth century. It is also a written monument to friendship and trust—qualities we can all learn from.

Imprisoned in 1943 at the age of sixteen for crimes he most likely didn't commit, Johnny Bragg was sentenced to six consecutive life terms, or 594 years, in state prison. With the support of Tennessee governor Frank Clement—who was elected to office in 1952 and who would become Bragg's close friend and confidant—Bragg's singing quintet, the Prisonaires, became an unprecedented chart-topping music act. The Prisonaires would also become Clement's showcase for his campaign on prison reform and civil rights.

In 1953 Bragg recorded his first of seven sessions at the legendary Sun Records studio for producer Sam Phillips. His musical influence would touch, among many others, Elvis Presley—who was present that first session and who became a close friend—Hank Williams, Burl Ives, Ernest Tubbs, and the Jordanaires.

This and more are to be found in this intimately researched book. The power of music, to teach and heal, lives on in the rich legacy of Johnny Bragg, Frank Clement, and the Prisonaires (Ed Thurman, William Stewart, Marcel Sanders, and John Drue). Johnny Bragg used to marvel at the equalizing power of music, even among *un*equals. I marvel at the power of the written word to bring such qualities to light, and at the talent of Jay Warner to transcribe it with such power and conviction. Warner proves, once again, that music is the universal language.

Introduction

In 1988 a fire destroyed a large portion of my home. The rebuilding was a nightmare and, to take my mind off these domestic disasters and the running of my company, I threw myself into a new book project.

For three years, I researched and wrote what became *The Billboard Book of American Singing Groups*. It was a history that hadn't been written and something I became obsessed with. When I had time to step back I re-read the work, cover to cover. For the first time, one seemingly small story that I'd had little information on stood out as the most unique among the four hundred acts I'd written about. It was the story of the Prisonaires.

I spent a month calling all my collector, author, and music historian friends for information on the group's lead singer, Johnny Bragg. Everyone had little bits of data but no one knew how to find Bragg. The search became more intriguing with each call. Fragment by fragment I learned about the Prisonaires' connection with Elvis and with other music legends, their hit single, and their fascinating role in Southern politics at the dawn of the civil rights era.

Eventually, a friend at ASCAP found a telephone number for Bragg. I called but he didn't want to talk. After three calls, he put me in touch with his attorney Don Hildebrand. (I learned that over the years he'd had plenty of attorneys.)

I had a few conversations with Hildebrand. I earned some credibility by sending a package of press clippings about my work and we made some legal arrangements about rights to Johnny's story. Then Don and I began to strike up a friendship, which led to a bonanza of details about Johnny, and I decided that I wanted to do a book on Johnny's life.

Don instructed his client to talk to me and to tell me anything I wanted to know. We had one two-hour conversation and I was overwhelmed by Bragg's stories. Finally, I went to visit Johnny.

We met at Hildebrand's office in Nashville. At the time I'd only seen pictures of Johnny with the group, from his muscular, youthful days. Now he was chunky, with a craggy face and bald head. But he was boyish and enthusiastic, and eager to tell his story. His heavy Southern accent made me strain to pick up and decipher his every word, but his memory was amazing.

He related incidents, some from more than fifty years ogo, as if he were describing this morning's breakfast. He pulled out a scrapbook of clippings and photos of himself as a young convict with the Prisonaires and other cellmates, as well as photos with celebrities, which added a new and authoritative dimension to his story.

We hit it off immediately, even though he drove me crazy when he drifted away from the subject. I'd have to go back two or three times to get my original question answered while he offered new details, describing events I hadn't heard about that fascinated me.

I realized that this project would require an ongoing series of interviews, something I couldn't do in person. So I made an arrangement with Hildebrand: I would begin researching the story through other sources and interviews and, as I pieced things together, would send lists of questions to the lawyer for him to ask Johnny, and to document and tape. He was more than willing to assist in telling a story he'd been a part of for over twenty years.

Johnny can't read or write. So over the next four years we worked through a combination of my phone interviews and questions to

Johnny and his meetings with Hildebrand to answer my list of queries.

I did over sixty phone interviews with Johnny during the late 1990s. I asked him about the key people in his life: Warden James Edwards, Governor Frank Clement, Congressman Bob Clement (the governor's eldest son), and Anna Belle Clement O'Brien (the governor's sister). He spoke politely and respectfully of each, talked about how each one treated him, how a quality of each—their belief in God—made him feel respected by them even though he was a convict.

Though it is fashionable to be cynical about politicians, I am persuaded that despite his ego and his ambition, Governor Frank Clement was willing to undertake immense political risks because he believed, as a man of faith, in the perfectibility of humankind. Period. There seem to me to be very, very few political figures today with the kind of integrity Clement showed in befriending Johnny. This doesn't diminish Johnny's bravery or his talent; it means that Clement gave Johnny the opportunity to be extraordinarily brave and to grow as an artist and as an individual.

I know Johnny understands all of this. In the time I've known him, I've never once heard him complain about the way he was treated. He seems remarkably unscarred by his early life. And despite Johnny having spent more than twenty-five years in prison, I have never heard him curse.

In reading this story you will probably experience, as I did in researching it, more than a few moments of disbelief. The life of Johnny Bragg and the members of the Prisonaires—half in the spotlight of celebrity, half in the shadows of the penitentiary—doesn't seem probable.

Again and again, one thinks there must be some embellishment or misunderstanding. Even more challenging to one's faith in Johnny are the stories of his encounters and conversations with great artists, political figures, and major players in the history of American music. Since I liked Johnny and knew that he had some remarkable accomplishments, I was willing to cut him some slack when he told me about meetings with Elvis, with George Wallace, with Harry Truman. "He doesn't read or write," I'd say to myself, "he belongs to an oral tradition. He's an old guy living in a romanticized past. He's trying to impress me."

And then, as I researched everything from newspapers, magazines, and books to liner notes and prison records, as I talked with other scholars of popular culture, as I interviewed utterly reliable witnesses such as Congressman Bob Clement, Warden James Edwards, and Anna Belle Clement O'Brien, I'd hear the same stories, often in greater detail. And I'd realize that one of the most miraculous things about Johnny Bragg was that, in a world filled with eccentrics and geniuses, he never had any idea just how remarkable he was.

YANK: Sure! Lock me up! Put me in a cage!

Dat's de on'y answer yuh know. G'wan, lock me up!

POLICEMAN: What you been doin'?

YANK: Enuf to gimme life for! I was born, see?

Sure, dat's de charge.

—Eugene O'Neill, The Hairy Ape

BABB Music
BMI 2:27
Morris

Vocal
U-81

MY GOD IS REAL
PRISONAIRES
Confined To Tennessee State Prison
Nashville, Tenn.
189
MEMPHIS, TENNESSEE

Death of a Champion

chapter one

NOVEMBER 6, 1969. Though it was improbable that he should do so, Johnny Bragg survived the one man he thought indestructible, the one man he cared enough about to wish that he'd gone first. It was only appropriate therefore that he played a part in the ceremony the day Frank Clement was buried.

Clement was only forty-nine when he died in a car accident.

There was a throng of mourners under the unseasonably warm Tennessee sun as it pushed skyward over the Dickson Memorial Gardens cemetery. Spectators outnumbered the family members, friends, and supporters present for the funeral of the former Tennessee governor.

There were country music stars and there were dignitaries. Among the dignitaries present to honor the man whose flag-draped casket was about to be lowered into the ground were Tennessee's Governor Buford Ellington, U.S. Senators Albert Gore Sr. and Howard Baker Jr., several members of Congress, state legislators, and even some of Clement's former political rivals.

Frank Clement was a man whom many opposed fiercely because he had allied himself with forces that were destroying their world. It would not be an exaggeration to say that, though very much in the minority, there must have been people there who were glad to see Clement gone.

Only the solitary, stocky, Black figure of Bragg standing over the gravesite singing an impassioned "My God Is Real" brought unity of silence and purpose to those otherwise divisive attendees. He finished his rendition, sweat pouring from his face, and slowly and pensively began to walk away.

One of the mourners, an attractive White woman, stopped him. According to Bragg, Anna Belle Clement O'Brien, the dead man's sister, whispered, "The people lost a great governor, I lost my only brother, and you lost your best friend." Johnny Bragg says he nodded, accepted her hug, and moved back through the crowd as the Reverend Virgil Tipps read from the Scriptures.

As a Black quartet sang "How Great Thou Art," the Reverend Doyle Masters read from the Apocrypha because, he said, "it bridges the Old and New Testaments, and Clement's philosophy bridged the old and new political schools." A shrewd observation. By background, religion, temperament, Frank Clement was an old-time Southern politician. Politically, however, he was an unabashed liberal, a believer in racial justice and assistance to the disadvantaged, a progressive politician in an increasingly conservative state at the beginning of the civil rights era.

Then Masters delivered his eulogy. When a Southern senator began his "I remember Frank Clement . . ." remarks as if it were a campaign speech, the singer Johnny Bragg eased away from the crowd, walked down the hill, and drove off in his dinged and dirty, salmon-colored, 1957 Mercury convertible, arriving at his destination in less time than it takes to lower a coffin and fill in a burial sight.

It was true, no question, that the governor had been his best friend.

The Woodlawn Cemetery stood atop a low, rolling hill on the north side of Nashville; the Black side. Johnny pulled into the parking lot and walked toward the crest to yet another waiting gravesite. There was only a handful of mourners here, none of them famous or powerful. The Reverend Raymond Liggon had been extemporizing, waiting for the singer's arrival. He introduced Johnny, who this time sang "Amazing Grace" and sang it with conviction, finishing with his usual falsetto flourish.

Johnny's mind, however, remained elsewhere, on the first funeral, the death of Clement, the years he'd spent in weekly, sometimes daily, contact with him. He thought about all the prejudice and violence he'd survived in his own life, while this man who seemed to have it all was suddenly gone in an instant. That Bragg was alive and free and had been singing at his friend's funeral was indeed amazing.

When the mourners left, there was more to do. Johnny stripped off his jacket and tie, rolled up his sleeves, and joined two young laborers to fill in and pat down the dirt. His prematurely graying temples and deeply lined face were in stark contrast to the muscular torso of a forty-three-year-old—the number of years Johnny Bragg had actually spent on this earth.

As he worked, Johnny was still thinking about Frank's funeral and what a good friend Clement had been to him. But Johnny Bragg and Frank Clement had actually been more than friends; they had, in a sense, been partners.

Johnny's success had helped the governor advance his political/religious agenda. Bragg demonstrated that criminals could be rehabilitated, that men could overcome their sins and errors. The governor had made it possible for Johnny, against all odds, first to become a celebrated performer and writer and then to become a free man.

Johnny's achievements make up the more remarkable story—an insight into the radical reshaping of American culture that began after World War II and continues to the present—but Clement is also exceptionally noteworthy.

In him, his background, his left-of-center political programs and right-of-center religious beliefs, we see an American politician unique to his time and place. The fact that Bragg and Clement could form a mutually useful alliance in the mid-twentieth-century South is in itself extraordinary.

In America, indeed throughout the world, there has been over the past half century a redefinition of the relationships between races, between generations, between urban and rural areas. No story evokes that redefinition more clearly than that of Johnny Bragg and his singing group. And no story makes it clearer how, unlikely as it seems, a key agent of change in the creation of the modern world was music.

Got to Have Show Fare

IT IS APPALLING to realize that any American alive today could have endured the injustice and privation that Johnny Bragg endured. The economic boom of the 1920s only touched the upper and middle classes. Earnings for the Black families who lived in North Nashville averaged $15 to $25 a month, a huge percentage of which went toward paying rent to wealthy White landlords.

The bleak Negro section of North Nashville was made up of hundreds of shoddily built, unpainted, two-bedroom frame houses without indoor plumbing. The names of districts were unpretentious and accurate reflections of real poverty and squalor—Hell's

Half-Acre, Mud Flats, and Black Bottom. One of the flats on Herman Street was the domain of Wade and Maybelle Bragg. Wade earned $6 a week as a Nashville, Chattanooga, and St. Louis (NC&St.L.) Railway freighthouse handler. Maybelle was a hard-working housemaid and mother of two young boys, Wade Jr. and James, and eldest child, Dorothy.

Their fourth child, John Henry, was born on a steamy morning May 6, 1926. Wade waited on the porch, smoking a corncob pipe, as he had during the birth of the first three children. This delivery was less fortunate. Maybelle died in childbirth.

It is difficult enough to escape such economic circumstances as theirs. For Johnny Bragg, who came into the world handicapped and motherless, the odds were inestimably longer.

Johnny says he was born blind. The local doctor told Wade that nothing could be done. He needed constant care. Wade was working twelve hours a day, six days a week, so for a few years Johnny was sent to Grandma Parthenia Jordan's home, along with Wade Jr., James, and Dorothy, and then at age three went with his brothers to live with his Aunt Mattie and Uncle Gus Haines. Gus was pastor of the Haines Baptist Church, next door to Wade's house. From an early age, Johnny was praying and singing gospel music.

At the Haines' the three boys shared one room and one bed. They saw their father on Sundays, when he would spend time riding herd over his brood. Johnny remembers: "He was tough but fair. . . . He was a Christian man, but he would let you know that he was boss."

Johnny never sang in the church choir but he managed to sing everywhere else. He remembers vividly the visits to his doctor. "When I was a little boy, I always loved that gospel music. I loved any kind of music. . . . I was born blind and the doctor used to sit me on a table and had me singin' to him. Some of the songs was 'My Blue Heaven' and 'What You Goin' To Do When the Rent Come 'Round?'"

At the age of six, Johnny inexplicably began to see. He calls it a miracle. Healthy, he now became one of the boys, a lively rambunctious child. By his own report he was likable, helpful, and good-natured to family and neighbors, yet somewhat trouble-bent, vexatious, and always willing to take a dare. He did what he felt like doing, whatever the consequences.

Years later he recalls, "Back in the slavery days, so to speak . . . my people would try to whup me, like when I did somethin' wrong they would whup you back then. The neighbors would whup you too if you got in trouble. That's when you got a whuppin', and when you went home you'd get another whuppin'."

He attended Head Elementary School, but Johnny willingly admits, "I didn't get much education. I didn't care anythin' about it. Far as I'm concerned, education wasn't nothin', y' know, just a thing called Joe."

Struggling to get by, Aunt Mattie and Grandma Parthenia had little time or energy to keep Johnny in school. They hoped the church would make all things right. As it turned out, they were wrong. But Johnny wasn't alone. Among Black children in Nashville in the year of his birth, eighteen hundred started first grade but only fifty-two ever saw a high school diploma.

When out of school, Johnny roamed the neighborhood with Bob, a vicious bulldog that only Johnny could control. Bob was a gift from Uncle Gus. "Bob was my friend," Johnny recalls. "We were together all the time. I used to take him around on a rope, but I couldn't turn him loose—he'd eat the neighborhood."

Bob, whom Uncle Gus called "the demon dog," wasn't allowed in the house. He had a doghouse in the backyard though, and sometimes Johnny slept there with him. It was profoundly upsetting to Johnny when Bob was found under the house after being poisoned. Johnny was only eight years old.

He claims to have been bad before he reached his teens, but there was also a kind side to Johnny Bragg. He liked to help older people in the neighborhood. "I love old people," Johnny says. "I used to help them in any way and every way I could, goin' to the grocery, cleanin' up their house, stealin' their empty Cocola bottles [to redeem for small change]. I got to have show fare [money for movies]. If I can't go to the show, then I can't be with the rest of the crowd."

Johnny's crowd was called the Black Legion, a youth gang of about two dozen kids from the neighborhood. Johnny's involvement with the gang gave him a feeling of self-worth that cruising solo never could. He was useful to the gang because he wouldn't back away from a dare. They dared him to break windows with a rock and he did. They dared him to throw bricks at chickens and there, too, he was the man for the job. "There was a bunch of us young boys that used to run together and, uh, we would kill the neighbors' chickens," Johnny recalls. "When they'd catch you killin' their chickens they would beat your ass to death, and wouldn't nothin' be done about it."

Johnny did a lot of fighting during his initiation into the gang. One memorable time he was bet that he couldn't beat up a White kid named Gene. "I was taught that a White man can't whup a Black man, just like the White guy was taught can't no nigger whup no White man." The fight brought him down a peg. "My two brothers were there so I fired off on 'im. I never will forget that. They tell me it was a half-hour later before I remembered anythin'. He knocked me out! But anyway, me and Gene became real good friends after that."

Through the years, as Johnny was growing up, the one thing that wasn't denied Southern Negroes was the music that came over the radio.

The first radio station in America was WWJ in Detroit, which went on the air in 1920. By 1924 legendary Black vocalist Bessie Smith had appeared on Memphis radio station WMC and the door to Black radio performers squeaked open. Groups like the Southernaires, the Golden Gate Quartet, and the Swan Silvertones made regular performance appearances on radio throughout the 1930s. By 1948 the first full-time broadcasting to African Americans came into being when WDIA in Memphis, Tennessee, focused its 50,000-watt antenna in the direction of the half-million Blacks in Tennessee, Missouri, Mississippi, and Arkansas.

The forerunner of rhythm and blues was race music. Where R&B (which doesn't really have a clear definition) could be considered Black pop, race music was its raw, sometimes less sophisticated precursor which was later mixed in various degrees with gospel, jazz, and blues to become R&B. Black disc jockeys, now famous blues singers such as B. B. King, Rufus Thomas, and Sonny Boy Williamson, as well as Howlin' Wolf on Radio WKUM, began playing the Black music that would soon become R&B. By the early 1950s over five hundred Black DJs were programming from most of the country's major cities.

Johnny's curiosity was satisfied with the simple flipping of the radio dial from Black to White and back to Black music stations again. In that way he was well-exposed to a wide variety of styles, from the passionate and pulsating gospel music of the church, created by acts like the Selah Jubilee Singers, the Norfolk Jubilee Quartet, and the Birmingham Quartet, to the rollicking race recordings of Fats Waller, Tampa Red, Robert Johnson, and Ella Fitzgerald, and the close harmonies of the Mills Brothers, the Charioteers, and Johnny's favorite, Bill Kenny and the Ink Spots. Kenny was a high tenor with a thrilling falsetto. Johnny spent many hours harmonizing on street corners and in alleyways with various vocal groups, developing a vocal style as similar as possible to Kenny's.

Johnny's love of singing had been further influenced during his youth by the presence of a local club. By age eleven he had begun collecting whiskey bottles for show fare by hanging around the Nashville Cotton Club on Heiman Street. "They used to let me in to get the cold-drink bottles and the whiskey bottles. I remember the last time I did that, I used to go to all the different guys' rooms, like the entertainers. Cab Calloway run me out of his room." (Calloway was an innovator in the early days of scat singing and jive talking, and later became a key transitional figure between the big band era and the emerging rhythm and blues.)

On one occasion Johnny found himself in a dressing room with a garbage can containing three large whiskey bottles. He scooped them up and took a step toward the door, when it swung wide and a beautiful woman stepped into the room. Johnny immediately knew from the marquee poster out front that it was Billie Holiday (one of the greatest female vocalists in jazz history). Still clutching the bottles he blurted out, "Uh, Miss Holiday, I wanna be a singer. Ya know,

I can sing." She asked him to sing something. Johnny began singing "A-Tisket, A-Tasket" while clutching the bottles and swaying to his own impromptu rhythm.

"Yeah, you can sing!" she agreed. "Now get your ass and my bottles outta here." The endorsement was something he cherished ever afterward. "I'll never forget that. She was a good lady, but she wasn't nothin' to play with."

HURT AND LONELY
(Johnny Bragg-Dorothy Wade)

Publisher:
ELBEJAY
Arrangement:
Bergen White
BMI
Time: 2:50

105   JOHNNY BRAGG

ELBEJAY Enterprises, Inc., P. O. Box 8905, Nashville, Tennessee 37211

Six Times Ninety-Nine

NOT QUITE DRAFT age, World War II barely touched Bragg. In the late 1930s, Wade Bragg had married Mary Ellstar and regrouped his family under one roof in the first low-income housing project in Nashville's Black neighborhood.

But having the family united with a new stepmother still didn't prevent Johnny from doing pretty much as he pleased. He avoided school and spent his time going to movies. He had several minor brushes with the law. At thirteen he was arrested and charged with taking drinks from a soft-drink truck. That time he was released. As a fourteen-year-old he served a month and a day in the State Training and Agricultural School at Pikeville for riding in a stolen auto. He was arrested later that same year by the FBI for, of all things, vagrancy. That time, too, he was released.

Most of the girls Johnny knew attended Baptist or Methodist churches and were closely tied to home and traditional values. Still, some were feeling and expressing their passions. Jenny Price, a neighbor from across the street, particularly appealed to Johnny. The two had been investigating each other sexually for almost six years. She was his favorite and his downfall.

This is how Johnny tells it: One day when he was sixteen Johnny came by Jenny's house to find her sexually involved with his friend Chester. "What the hell you think you're doin'?" Johnny yelled. Jenny pushed Chester to the floor and told Johnny, "Whatever I want, I ain't yours."

"Well, you ain't his," Johnny objected. Jenny then jumped off the bed, tackled Johnny, and flailed at his chest. Chester sat naked on the bare bedroom floor, watching the two teens wrestle. Jenny not only held her own, but she also landed a right fist in Johnny's eye and gave him a larger-than-life lip. The sight of this naked, well-endowed sixteen-year-old, punching her fully clothed boyfriend and rolling across the floor, had Chester in stitches. His was the last laugh for a long time. Johnny, realizing he was getting the worst of the fight, finally stormed out, kicking a soup can all the way to his front door.

When Jenny's parents came home from work, they found her banged up; she had to come up with an excuse. Her parents stormed over to the Bragg home and confronted Wade. Johnny heard every word: "That boy of ya's raped my Jenny," Mrs. Price screamed in Wade's face.

"Which boy? I got three, y' know," he shouted back.

"John Henry did it."

Mr. Price cut in, "My little girl said so."

Jenny, fearful of being caught in a consensual, promiscuous situation in her own home with Chester, had accused Johnny before he could accuse her. And she had to stick to her story, especially about how Johnny beat her up. "If I beat you up so bad, how come I'm in worse shape?" Johnny objected, missing the whole point. Jenny shouted, "Cuz you deserve to be!"

Meanwhile, eight or nine voices from the Bragg and Price households, in varying degrees of contentious thrust and parry, scarcely noticed when Mrs. Price stomped down the hall, ripped the pay phone from its receiver, and dialed the police. Tempers were hot and soon there was no going back. Two burly White policemen showed up soon after. Barely before the bewildered Johnny had time to profess his innocence, and in the midst of the two families hurling obscenities at each other, the police hustled him out the front door with Wade in hot pursuit.

The distraught father begged the lawmen to let his son go, but one cop brushed him aside and threatened him with obstruction of justice. Johnny was hurled into the car, taken to the downtown precinct, and thrown into a cell with another teen. Fingerprinting, the reading of rights, or a call to a lawyer would all have to wait for another age.

Johnny's first night in jail reaffirmed his perception of race relations. His cellmate, a gangly seventeen-year-old named Horace, began by asking Johnny what he had done.

"Didn't do nothin'," Johnny insisted.

"What'd they say you did?" Horace persisted.

"Said I raped my girlfriend, but I didn't. My friend Chester was foolin' with her and I caught 'em."

"So you beat her and she gave you up, huh?"

"She beat me better."

"Yeah, you look it, but she had no choice. I seen it all before. Prob'ly some marks on her. Either she admits she fucked your friend or blames a rape on you," Horace decided. He had learned to be a realist.

"What are you, a lawyer?" Johnny fired back.

"Nope, I'm a bike thief."

"They don't lock you up for that."

"It was a White boy's bike," Horace explained.

The next day Johnny was visited by Nashville detectives. They spent about five minutes in his cell, politely questioning him, and ten minutes more beating him.

As Johnny has told it, probably a hundred times, "Jenny said I tried to rape her and that I jumped on her. I didn't jump on her, I caught a friend of mine with her, you see, and we had a lot of words, and me and Jenny fought."

The detectives weren't really interested in his story, they just wanted a quick confession. When it wasn't forthcoming they smacked him around and left, one detective mumbling, "There's more than one way to skin a nigger."

Two or three days later the detectives began parading strangers past Johnny's cell. They were all Black women of varying ages and all seemingly nervous and impatient. He remembers: "They all were bigger 'n me. I'da had to get on a chair to attack one of 'em." Johnny himself was not quite five feet seven and skinny as a rail. About two weeks into his stay, the detectives brought a White woman to his cell and the scenario played out the same way it had with the others.

It turned out that these women were all former rape victims whose cases remained open because the rapist had not yet been identified. That is, not until they were pressured into identifying Bragg. It was not uncommon for White detectives in the South to "clean up the books" in such a way, and the police were certainly ready and eager to accuse Johnny in any outstanding rape cases.

Though family members came to visit the accused, there was little they could do to console him. A trial date still had not been set and it seemed that when some good news was delivered one day, it was reversed by bad news the next. On a late winter day, Wade and Johnny's brother James paid a visit to the jail. They sat down at a rectangular table in the visitation room, with a guard standing no more than a few feet away. Wade felt they had some good news. James had gotten Jenny to tell the truth, and her family dropped the charges. He assured Johnny that everything was going to be all right.

But the authorities had not bothered to notify James and Wade of the seven additional rape charges brought against Johnny. Wade argued on Johnny's behalf. It did no good.

Johnny finally went to trial in the late winter of 1943. His lawyer, a weary-looking public defender, told Wade that he might be able to get Johnny out in nine months but if they tried to dispute the charges Johnny might get the electric chair. The Bragg family was thoroughly intimidated.

Even though the White woman's case was thrown out, the six Black women all stuck by their stories. Following his lawyer's advice, Johnny did not testify on his own behalf. An all-White, all-male jury found him guilty and he was sentenced to six ninety-nine-year sentences without possibility of parole. Sixteen-year-old, directionless John Henry Bragg now had a direction, albeit an undesirable one.

Cell Five, Walk Ten

chapter four

THE TENNESSEE STATE Prison at Nashville, built just before the turn of the century, sat on the south bank of the Cumberland River, three miles from the center of town. It was an awesome fortress of the forgotten, with a Gothic-tower entrance faced in Pikeville sandstone and weathered white brick that the full-blown four seasons of the Tennessee Valley had shaded into a depressing and austere gray.

In the early 1940s, it held nearly fourteen hundred inmates. Johnny Bragg joined them on his seventeenth birthday. A young Black lifer in the old South, he seemed unlikely ever to reenter the world. He was at an absolute dead end.

His introduction to prison realities came with his first-day encounter with Deputy Warden Swafford. He was called "Scrap Iron," Johnny says, "cuz he was tough, very tough, and he was the whippin' boss at that time, and when I went before him he told me not to get outta line. He said, 'Don't no nigger run this place, I'm the boss here. You're gonna be treated just like everybody else. I don't care how young you are, if you mess up I'm gonna beat your ass to death. You can get ready for it.'"

Bragg was assigned to cell number five on Walk Ten, where he resided the whole time he was there. It was a standard six-foot-by-eight-foot cell, with three walls and a latticelike door that seemed to block more light than it let in. The door's two-inch-wide crossbars—four vertical, thirteen horizontal—created a checkerboard effect that would play tricks on his eyes if he stared at it too long. Opposite the door was a toilet and sink. A dirty oak cupboard faced the bed. The upper bunk had already been claimed by a small-time thief. There were fleas and lice everywhere.

Bragg was a young man without a future or much of a past. "I didn't know 'bout no ninety-nine years. Ninety-nine years wasn't nothin' but a day to me cuz I didn't know no better."

He was too young to have much he could hold on to from the outside—a pathetically small frame of reference that centered mostly on being outdoors as a kid: the streets he'd roamed with his beloved "demon dog," Bob; the golf course at the Bellemeade Country Club where he'd caddied for movie money; the baseball field; the porch of Jenny's house, which he'd rather *not* think about now. And there was his family: his two older brothers, now in the army on the European front; his dad; his sister, Dorothy, and her great cooking.

In the penitentiary personal memories and thoughts got lost, superseded by prison routine. Inmates rose at 6:15 A.M., dressed and mustered for inspection, and were in the mess hall by 7:00 A.M. for breakfast. There were two huge dining areas, one for Negroes and one for Whites—the two groups segregated for meals and sleeping. The kitchen's enormous cooking kettles could prepare a hundred gallons of coffee, sixteen bushels of cooked vegetables, five hundred pounds of meat, and fifty gallons of soup. It stuck to the ribs but it was nothing like home.

A half-hour for breakfast and then the morning's work. Lunch was at 11:30 A.M. and by noon most were back at work. Some inmates, on a rotating basis, would be allowed to play baseball and as many as two games an afternoon could be completed on the field. Exercises and running were also an integral part of the afternoon activities. Supper was at 5:00 P.M. and by 5:30 all the prisoners went back to their cellblocks. Lights out was at 9:00 P.M. Routine was enforced by two twelve-hour shifts of fifty or sixty of penology's best and worst guards.

Johnny was assigned to a work detail in the clothes factory, a comparatively comfortable job. All inmates dressed in loose-fitting, gray-and-white striped shirts and pants. He made shirts on the second floor, taught the craft by an inmate named Tyrone. It was there that he met a man he recollects only as Sam, one of many who gave him some perspective on life inside. Before being sent to prison, Sam had been working cleaning floors in a slaughterhouse. Prison work was a step up in the world for him.

"Where'd you work?" Sam asked.

"I used to clean houses of old people . . ."

"What'd you steal?" asked Sam.

"What makes you think I stole somethin'?" Bragg shot back.

"You're here, aren't you?" Sam said.

"Well, I took their Cocola bottles, only the used ones, see . . . "

"You in the pen for stealin' Coca Cola bottles?" one of the men asked.

Johnny was offended. "I'm in the pen for nothin'!"

Suddenly two guards dragged a prisoner from behind Bragg and pulled him up the stairs to the third floor.

Johnny whispered, "What's upstairs?"

Sam said with resignation, "The end of the line."

Prisoners lived for visiting day. The reception area where inmates met their relatives was simply a large room with chairs and tables. Convicts sat on opposite sides of tables from family or friends, surrounded by armed guards who paid attention to everything.

Johnny's regular callers were usually his sister, Dorothy, and Grandma Parthenia, who would bring him some homecooking. On occasion his father would come by, and these were both the highest and lowest moments of Johnny's visitations. Wade could only talk around the situation. "Ya brother James, he's workin' at St. Thomas Hospital now, ya know." Wade could barely make eye contact with his youngest son.

Prison did not transform him; Johnny Bragg the prisoner remained aimless. Any diversion would do. Once he came upon an old worn length of a belt and would pop it skyward in the yard like a whip. The guards nicknamed him "Zorro."

Boredom and hopelessness made him reckless. As he recalls years later: "I was young and I had the attitude, when I first went to prison, I didn't care what they'd do. I'm just gonna make myself at home cuz ain't nobody to live to get out anyhow. Everybody in there is goin' to die. That's what I thought. I was just a silly boy and I didn't know no better." The guards needed little provocation. To most of them there were only two types of prisoners, niggers and White trash, and both were treated with equal disdain when it came to physical punishment.

On a few occasions Johnny refused to work. Then he was beaten. The first time this happened—it was his worst beating—he had been slow to react at the shirt shop. He was grabbed by the neck and marched up the stairs to the third floor. The room was dusty and bare except for support beams, each with a metal ring attached about six feet off the ground. Two more guards followed the first and tied Johnny's hands to a center beam ring. He could hear the whoosh of leather belts being pulled through the belt loops of their pants. He heard the sound again and two buckles bit into his back. He tried to arch away from the beam, practically jerking his arms out of their sockets. Blood oozed down his back and through his ripped shirt. He was beaten unconscious.

Not everyone rebelled in the same way. Other inmates mutilated themselves. "Inmates were cuttin' their arms," Johnny says, "cuz they couldn't take the tass [being beaten]. If they get messed up so bad they had to get to the hospital, they didn't have to worry about tass."

It was several years before Johnny began to pay attention to the informal gospel singing groups throughout the prison. Most of them sang the sort of music Johnny had learned at his uncle's church. He made it a point to be nearby when any of the three or four quartets would practice in the courtyard, auditorium, or lunchroom. In time Johnny went from being a curious bystander to an ardent admirer.

He began by being a critic of the singers and then, perhaps subconsciously, to plan how he could make his mark among them. He noted the instability of the groups, their lack of discipline, the frequent changes in their membership. The rehearsals he observed were unfocused, full of false starts and silliness. Nevertheless, the singers had influence. Johnny's workmate Sam, who was one of the singers, told him that guards were lenient toward them. "I started singin' spirituals with a couple of guys in the yard. Neal [Assistant Deputy Warden Bill Neal] likes music so he don't let the guards hassle us."

But Johnny didn't appreciate their work. He truly didn't understand why these groups couldn't be as polished as the singers he had listened to when he was a kid in church. He was beginning to discover that he knew more about music than his fellow prisoners. Johnny still remembers a conversation he had with Sam:

"I love those Ink Spots," he said.

"What about the Mills Brothers, they're somethin' else," Sam replied.

"Yeah, and Perry Como," Johnny enthused.

"Who?" Sam asked.

"Perry Como—White man, mellow sound." Unlike other Black prisoners, Johnny also knew White pop singers. The fact that he had more knowledge of music to draw on was one of the things that set him apart from the others.

Sam belonged to one of the better quartets, headed by veteran inmate Edward Lee Thurman, a gangly six-foot-plus Black man with a narrow, gaunt face. They were practicing in the yard one day when Johnny, shyly at first, joined in on one familiar spiritual and then another. Johnny was a strong tenor and finished with a solid C over high C. Sam introduced Johnny to lead singer Ed Thurman, baritone William Stewart, and tenor Charlie Moore.

Though he had no musical training, Johnny had always been able to sing harmony and possessed a natural ear for harmonic arrangement. The men were impressed with Johnny's voice and Johnny felt good.

Ed cut to the heart of the matter. "Restores your dignity, don't it?" He had read Johnny's mind. Bragg began to sing harmonies with the group whenever they practiced and he helped to rework harmony parts that had crumbled from lack of musical maintenance.

They were decent singers, favorably treated, but they were not angels and they'd had no luck. Ed had been twenty-three years old when he came to "Swafford's Graveyard," as the penitentiary was nicknamed, in August 1940. He was from Nashville and was serving a ninety-nine-year sentence for having shot and killed the man who killed his dog.

Ed was what they called a "headbolter," something like the cellblock enforcer or buffer for the guards. He had a desk on the ground floor of the block and helped the guards keep track of everyone. His key function was to stop the inmates from killing each other; fights were as common as the ever-present fleas, mosquitoes, and lice. Ed also held deep-seated religious beliefs and for several years had been leading Bible-study meetings.

The unnamed group's baritone, William Stewart, came from Hartsville, Tennessee. He played guitar, which set their group apart from the groups who sang a cappella. Handsome, with deep-set eyes and a pencil-thin mustache, Stewart was soft-spoken but laughed a lot and liked photography and drinking. He entered prison in December 1940 at the age of eighteen. One of eight children, he and three friends were charged with killing a White man with a fence rail. Though someone else admitted to the murder, Stewart pleaded guilty because his public-defender lawyer told him he would get the death penalty if he did not do so. From that moment on, William was destined to become another member of the nine-decades-and-nine club.

One day, when Sam had been sent to the dry cell (solitary) and didn't show for a laundry-room rehearsal, Ed went looking for a replacement. He found Johnny playing baseball. Paying no attention to the game, he walked into the outfield shouting, "You wanna sing? Sam's in the dry cell. If you wanna sing, we're in the laundry."

Johnny left the game on the run.

Sam, who had been Johnny's mentor, never resurfaced. What became of him? "Some prisoners, beaten so bad, ya know," Johnny says, "sometimes they killed inmates. No one knew what happened to 'em. Some had no families. Word was they had a accident, but we knew."

The quartet's performance was erratic at best. They practiced when they could, now and again, reaching a few musically satisfying peaks on a song or two like "Precious Lord." Johnny says of lead singer Thurman, "I had a lot of respect for Ed Thurman. He was my boss in a way, because he's the one that got me in the group."

They sometimes sang in a bathroom to take advantage of the echo effect off the walls, but their harmonies were drowned out by the sound of flushing toilets and the howls of a few dogs that lived in the prison.

For the quartet, singing was a buffer against the realities of prison life, a means of mental escape; Johnny felt that only his dreams were free. He says he could escape the boredom, the ugliness, and the beatings by singing and writing songs. He could not put words to paper or a tune to sheet music, but he could work and rework melodies and lyrical images in his head. The idea that he should write songs came to him in the late 1940s during a disagreement.

Johnny was singing in his lower bunk when his cellmate said, "Hey, don't you know no other songs? You drivin' me crazy with them same old spirituals."

Johnny yelled back, "Whatcha want me to do, invent a song?"

"Yeah," the inmate countered, "Write somethin' bluesy or country or somethin'!"

Johnny confessed, "I can't write."

"Can you remember?" the man asked. "Write somethin' in your head and we'll get somebody to write it down for ya when you got it right."

This was the first great paradox of Johnny's life: He might never have become an artist, a man who made his mark in the world, had he not first been a lost soul.

Birth of the Prisonaires

BY THE LATE 1940s, radios—owned or controlled by the guards—proliferated in the pen. Country-western, gospel, blues, and even pop music could be heard throughout the penitentiary.

Johnny's songwriting continued, on occasion aided by one or more of the various literate inmates. They would help him translate his personally crude code into a lyric line or two. Johnny recalls trying to write songs back then: "I'd pick up an old piece of paper off the ground. If a song had [the word] 'heart' in it, all I could put in it was maybe a 't' or a 'h'. If there was a 'girl' in it, I'd put 'g'. I wrote lots of songs that way."

Johnny's passion for music didn't end with group practices. He'd sing alone in his cell, sometimes for hours at a time. The convicts within earshot were generally tolerant, but as he tried to get a phrase right, starting and stopping over and over again, he remembers other prisoners becoming irritated, shouting, "Shut up, Johnny. Sing it all the way through or don't sing it 't all." But he wasn't about to stop.

Then one day he discovered that he could muffle his voice in a way that had additional benefits. "I had a ol' metal washbucket, see. I could put this big bucket over my head to keep down the sound and it'd give me a echo like a microphone, and I could hear my voice real good," Johnny remembers.

The sight of a convict standing in his cell singing with a bucket covering everything down to his shoulders, elicited remarks like "What you all doin' in there, boy?" from each shift of guards. One guard even wanted to send him to the infirmary for questioning, but most tolerated it as a personal eccentricity. The guards began to call him "Bucket Head" or "Bucket Mouth." They may have thought he was crazy, but they liked his singing.

One Sunday, late in the day, the foursome was singing in the courtyard. They were in particularly good form as they wailed their way through a gospel standard while a guard looked on. Another guard passed by and asked, "Who are they?" The first sentry bellowed loudly and sarcastically, "They're the damn Mills Brothers! Who'd you think they are? They're just the prisoners."

Johnny overheard the exchange. When the group finished to go inside he said to Thurman, "You know, we should have a name." The unsolicited suggestion from the guard had made him think. Wanting something with more dignity than "the prisoners," Johnny volunteered, "How's The Prisonaires?"

Thurman nodded, Moore smiled, and Stewart said, "Sounds fine." With that less-than-exuberant but unanimous approval, the Prisonaires were born.

There is a distinction, hard to define, between folk art and high art. One sign of it may be self-consciousness. Some artists are more aware than others of what they do. They can think through changes in their work.

By the mid-century, musical styles began to interact. Radio broke down musical genres and racial barriers and merged them. Artists subconsciously combined forms to create their new sounds. It was true of Elvis, as it was later true of the Beach Boys and the Beatles.

With so much secular music on radio, it was inevitable that Thurman's group would begin crossing boundaries from their roots in gospel and spiritual music. Johnny remembers vividly the first of this musical strategizing at breakfast in early 1950. He and William Stewart were working their way through the morning grits when Ed set his tray down.

"Charlie has given up."

"Given up what, eatin'?" Johnny asked.

"Singin', at least with us," Ed said.

"Why?" William asked.

"Says he won't sing secular songs. Says what we're doin' is blasphemy."

"And that from a man who robbed old ladies!" Johnny laughed.

"Yeah, but he never hurt no one," Ed argued.

"And he never robbed nobody on a Sunday," William added.

They tried to persuade Moore to change his mind but he wanted nothing more to do with them. His defection could have led to a total breakup of the Prisonaires, but Johnny had different plans.

Having plans at all was a major maturation for him. His days of aimless behavior were replaced by his motivation and confidence not only as a singer, but now also as a self-appointed leader of the group. Johnny began recruiting new members. He went through the prison listening to anyone and everyone who could hold a note. Keeping a nucleus of himself, Ed Thurman, and William Stewart, for some time the fourth spot became a revolving door of anonymous convicts.

The Prisonaires were always available and they were pressed into service in the prison anytime an event needed solemnizing. The prison chaplain, for instance, began to ask death row inmates if they'd like some of the boys to sing for them before execution. If requested to do so, the Prisonaires would be brought to the death house on the north side of the prison courtyard. There they would sing a spiritual and provide a moment of distraction for the condemned man while the chaplain, warden, and guards looked on. Then the man to be executed would be strapped to "Sparky," the death row guards' nickname for the electric chair.

"It was a terrible thing. Some of these boys were charged with murder. Majority of them was murder, majority of them was Black, and it was a sad, sad situation," Johnny recalls. Few of the condemned went quietly. Many, most even, protested their innocence to the end.

"Some of those guys got the chair that wasn't s'posed to get the chair. I got educated, so to speak, in prison when we did all the entertainment for the death house." The singing of the Prisonaires was often more effective than the chaplain's prayers, and many men in the holding cell broke down as they heard the music.

"I never'll forget, there was this tough White boy, Sam Kelly. They had him for four or five murders, bank robberies and things, and they asked him, 'You all want them to come up and sing for ya?' Sam, he didn't care. 'Ya can send someone to sing if ya wanna. Doesn't make much difference,'" Johnny remembers him saying. But as he was being led from the holding cell, he had a change of mind.

"He wanted me to sing a song just before he went down. He wanted 'Amazing Grace,'" Johnny says, "and I remember tryin' to sing it. I didn't know all the words to the song, but I sang what I knew and he cried like a baby."

Almost everyone—guards, officials, medics, and singers alike— left the area as soon as the execution was finished. Johnny often remained behind with Raymond Bryant, the worker assigned to clean up.

"I used to help take them outta the chair. I used to help Raymond Bryant. . . . A lot of times he needed some help and I told him I would help him. I'd unstrap 'em and he'd clean it up."

Sudden death is hard to comprehend and Johnny had to find a way to accept it.

"I would sit in the chair and I'd go on playin' 'I don' wanna die, I don' wanna die' . . . silly stuff, ya know?"

On one occasion after Johnny had vented, Ray said, "We're all gonna die. Maybe you'll be lucky enough not to have it happen this way. Anyway, you got a lot of years ahead of ya."

Johnny knew, though he was young, healthy, and had discovered his vocation as a singer, that he would also be in prison for the rest of his life.

As a way of reducing tensions among the inmates and giving them something to look forward to, the warden occasionally allowed musicians to perform at the penitentiary. From country artists like Little Jimmy Dickens, Ernest Tubbs, Red Foley, and Roy Acuff, to blues singers Muddy Waters and Louis Jordan, the Tennessee State Prison became a stop on the touring schedules of many nationally known acts.

Long before a carnival huckster named Colonel Tom Parker came to prominence managing hip-swiveling sensation Elvis Presley, he was procuring talent such as Carl Smith, George Morgan, and Cowboy Copas for Swafford's Graveyard. Add those acts to the regular spiritual performers the prison's chaplain could corral, such as the Jordanaires, and the state pen started looking like the Grand Ole Opry with bars.

There was also organized entertainment from the inside. The Prisonaires were invited to perform at the prison variety shows more than once, thanks to Bob Brassell, the White inmate who directed the events. Had Johnny Bragg been living in the world outside, he might never have had so many opportunities to perform.

During the summer of 1951 a new inmate (and former convict) came to Thurman's attention. Easygoing Marcel Sanders had a habit of singing in a low, rich bass voice over his meals in the commissary. The twenty-seven-year-old Sanders didn't look as though he had the heft of a bass. He was tall and thin like Thurman, with a large nose and big ears.

Ed and Johnny could hear him from the other end of the long, twenty-man table singing "Ol' Man River." He reminded them of Jimmy Ricks (legendary bass singer considered by many to be the greatest group bass of all time) of the Ravens. When Ed, Johnny, and William approached him in a corridor after lunch, Marcel was wary; he had previously been in the penitentiary from April 1950 to April 1951 for felonious assault.

Johnny remembers the encounter:

"You sure get deep," William said.

"I can go deeper," Marcel responded, after he realized that William was talking about singing.

"We're called the Prisonaires," Ed offered. "We sing for fun."

"And for shows," Johnny chimed in. "And we ain't got no bass."

Marcel lowered his voice and responded, "Well, if you want a bass, you got one now."

Soon afterwards, an unexpected fifth piece fit into the Prisonaires puzzle when auditions were held for another of Brassell's productions. As the quartet looked on, John Edward Drue Jr., a twenty-five-year-old tenor, stepped onto the stage and wowed all within earshot with his rendition of the Ink Spots' "If I Didn't Care," coincidentally one of Johnny's favorites. Johnny was listening. Though his own singing style borrowed from the Ink Spots' lead singer, Bill Kenny, he recognized that Drue was a serious talent and he wanted to work with him.

Johnny turned to Ed and said, "Ya know, if we sound good with four, we'd knock 'em out with five." Marcel Sanders agreed. "I'm just glad he ain't a bass."

Drue, also known as Junior, liked cars and hard liquor and was serving a three-year sentence for larceny. He had been jailed in January 1951 for car theft stemming from an extended car ride in October 1950. Seems he took a test drive in an inebriated condition and when he returned two hours later he was arrested. He pleaded guilty on advice of his counsel.

The Prisonaires had become a first-time fivesome, and they were good. By 1951 the group was making regular treks to the prison auditorium. Johnny had been reassigned from the clothing factory to take charge of the cleanup crew in the assembly hall, which allowed him to have a small dressing room backstage as an office and allowed for regular rehearsal use of the stage.

The group's stylistic development was unconventional from the day it became a quintet. Owing greatly to Johnny's influence, the group went beyond spiritual and gospel songs to blues, pop, and hillbilly. Johnny's songs and song ideas began forcing the group to extend its range. Artists brought in to perform for the convicts were sometimes surprised to hear, from both guards and trustees helping set up for their shows, that they ought to hear some of the songs one of the prisoners had written.

Johnny knew, even then, that it was the oddity, the novelty of a convict songwriter that began to attract attention: "Word got around there was a nigger who could write any kind of song."

Before he knew it, Johnny says, artists including Little Jimmy Dickens, Roy Acuff, Gene Autry, Burl Ives, Cecil Gant, and Ernest Tubbs were reportedly picking his brain.

Johnny Bragg's unique life needed no dramatization but, to some extent, elements of an encounter here or there may have been embellished.

One persistent tale told by Bragg involves legendary country vocalist Hank Williams. Johnny's account is that at a prison event one Saturday night in the early '50s the Prisonaires were harmonizing in a backstage dressing room, waiting their turn onstage, when Williams appeared backstage and began tuning his guitar.

He exchanged compliments with them. Four of the group then left to watch the show but Johnny stayed behind, sensing an opportunity. He asked Williams if he ever sang songs written by other people.

"Depends," Hank said, continuing to tune. "You one of those other people?"

"I been doin' some writin'," Johnny said. "You wanna hear the song I wrote?"

"Sure, I got five minutes," Williams said.

Johnny clasped his hands together and began his a cappella version.

Hank initially listened out of curiosity, but as the song unfolded he leaned forward intently as Johnny wailed from his heart, finishing not with an expected flourish but a somber, descending tone.

"That's real nice son. Best you get on stage with your group now," he said.

"Well, thanks for listening," Johnny said dejectedly as he turned for the door.

Williams, apparently thinking better of it, said, "Son, it's a five-dollar song. You get it written out and I'll give you five dollars for it."

Five dollars in cash was a nice piece of change for a prisoner. In those days a working inmate earned only two to five dollars for an entire week. "You got a deal, Mr. Williams!" Johnny exclaimed, and raced to the stage just in time to join the group.

"Where you been?" Marcel asked.

"Mr. Hank, he just offered me five dollars for my song!"

"Well, if that don't make you the five-dollar man," Junior said, not realizing he was giving the writer a nickname that would stick for years to come.

The story can't be documented one way or another, but it is a possible event given practices in the music business of the '50s.

Music historian and author Colin Escott wrote, "Among the songs Bragg claims to have sold was 'Your Cheatin' Heart,' and it is at least possible that Williams bought the genesis of the song from Bragg as he bought other songs that he made uniquely his own."

Years later, the multimillion-selling hit under Hank Williams' solo writing credit tempered Johnny's original enthusiasm.

"I wrote 'Your Cheatin' Heart.' Hank Williams didn't write 'Your Cheatin' Heart,'" Johnny states flatly. "I'd get all these songs in my mind. I had different versions for every song, and four or five different ways to sing 'em. Different words for the same song. 'Your Cheatin' Heart,' I had two or three different versions. You see, it was just a gift from God, but I wouldn't let anyone know I couldn't read or write. So I'd get by myself and when I'd get the song exactly right, I'd have somebody write it down for me. Now Hank, as soon as he heard that song, he wanted that song."

Music was filling Johnny's days and nights.

He remembers: "I thought about the music so strong that when I went to sleep I'd go to dances in my dreams, and every song they'd play seemed like a new song. I woke up in the mornin' and started writin' 'em. I had somethin' like a vision; I did a lot of prayin' back then. I really came face to face with God when I was incarcerated. I asked to meet all these different people and I met everybody. I said, 'Let me organize a singin' group, Lord. I want this group to travel all over and sing God's praises.'"

Excellorec
Music Co.
BMI

Popular
Vocal Group
Time 2:50

LOVE YOU—LOVE YOU—LOVE YOU
(Johnny Bragg)
THE MARIGOLDS
45-2061

Changing of the Guard

chapter six

JOHNNY BRAGG'S GREATEST gift may
have been a friendship, developed over several decades, with a White
man—a complex, principled White man whose star was rising in 1952.

As Johnny and the group worked to polish and hone the Prisonaires' sound, they could never have imagined the way that state and
national politics would soon change their lives forever.

For decades, Tennessee law stated that gubernatorial balloting must be
held every two years. A candidate could succeed himself for three consecutive terms (six years) and, after being out of office for one term,
could run again.

The first Tennessee governor of the 1950s, Gordon Browning, was rugged and contentious, a conservative Democrat who had been governor for six years total and was serving out his third two-year term, though only the last two had been consecutive. He combined a fiery temperament with a fierce stubbornness and prided himself on controlling state debt with a pay-as-you-go policy.

Browning's opponent in the Democratic primary was Frank G. Clement, a young, idealistic attorney. Clement was progressive, running on a platform of improved education, mental health reform, and reform of the state gasoline tax. His charm and idealism contrasted strongly with Browning and his machine. Clement, a six-foot-tall, blue-eyed Methodist, had wavy black hair, the features of a matinee idol, and the engaging smile of a career politician.

He loved music and liked to listen to his record collection whenever he could; it consisted mostly of hymns, religious quartets, and hillbilly tunes. He watched TV (which was new to the state and to the country) to improve his oratorical skills, studying the mannerisms and gestures of the singers and actors. His speaking voice could resemble every instrument in an orchestra, from a cello's sweet song to the clarion call of a trumpet. His oratorical abilities were a natural gift, but his diction was sharpened in early life by his "Aunt Dockie" Weems, an elocution teacher and noted college drama director who also coached his younger sister Anna Belle.

Anna Belle was always convinced her brother would go far. She especially amused the managers of Nashville's Capitol Chevrolet by accepting a job on the condition they'd give her a leave of absence "when my brother runs for governor."

Clement came from the railroad village of Dickson, a town of 2,200 people, about thirty miles west of Nashville. His birthplace was a back bedroom on the first floor of the unpretentious Halbrook Hotel, a stone's throw from the tracks of the NC&St.L. Railway, the same railroad for which Johnny Bragg's dad worked. Frank's father, Robert S. Clement, was city attorney in Dickson and his grandfather was J. A. Clement, a state senator.

But the Clements were not well-to-do and young Frank sold newspapers at an early age to help out. Even as a teenager Frank had displayed a keen sense of his future. He would often stop to speak with people on the street, stick out his hand with a simultaneous smile and the words "Frank Clement."

His sister Anna Belle, later a state congresswoman and a twenty-year member of the Tennessee State Senate, says with pride: "Frank told me when he was sixteen that he wanted to be governor of the state. I said, 'Why would you want to do that?' and he said, 'Because there are kids in my class who are smarter then I am but they can't afford the text books.' He felt their abilities were being wasted."

His special interest in mental health reform was heavily based on the experiences of an uncle who, when Frank Clement was a youth, was institutionalized because of a brain injury. In post–World War II Tennessee, mental institutions (as mental healthcare facilities were called then) were run by the same state agency that ran the prisons and there wasn't much of a difference between the two. Clement also felt it was wrong for elderly people to have to mortgage their homes just to receive government assistance, a position he would fight for in his first term as governor, guiding legislation through the state legislature and changing the law.

A Bible student since boyhood, Frank Clement's flamboyant style was a cross between the Reverend Billy Graham (of whom he became a close friend and follower) and the "give 'em hell" school of politics that President Harry S. Truman was famous for. Clement once said, "If you can't mix your politics and religion, there's something wrong with your politics." On January 16, 1953, Frank Goad Clement became the Volunteer State's new governor.

Clement had always been in a hurry. He passed the bar exam before finishing law school and was admitted to the bar with the highest exam mark among the 244 state applicants.

Upon graduation, Clement spent three months in the FBI training school in Quantico, Virginia, and became a special agent for the FBI by convincing them to lower their age requirement of twenty-three. From July 1942 through November 1943 he was a Chicago-based agent.

In 1943, realizing a political career would be helped by having military service on his record, Clement waived his draft-exempt FBI status to become Private Clement, and went on to earn the rank of first lieutenant while becoming commander of an MP battalion—the youngest company commander in his brigade.

On June 4, 1945, as World War II was drawing to a close, he was promoted to first lieutenant. His record stated that he was a rifle expert, submachine-gun expert, and carbine sharpshooter, but the closest he ever got to the fighting was his post at Camp Gordon, Texas.

When Frank was in law school at Vanderbilt University, he married Lucille Christianson, a petite, brown-eyed, blonde beauty. Her quiet nature was in stark contrast to the outgoing Clement. Lucille had studied violin and piano, inheriting her music sensibilities from her mother. She had dreamed of going to Hollywood to be a star ever since she was young, but her parents wouldn't permit it. From the day she married Frank she began a life of playing second fiddle to her husband's dreams and it made for a marriage that, though it was loving, wasn't always happy.

Clement returned to Dickson and private law practice after his discharge in 1946 and was named general counsel for the Tennessee Railroad and Public Utilities Commission. By 1950 Clement had resigned the government post to enter a law practice with his father, and served as state commander of the American Legion and state chairman for the March of Dimes until he ran for his first elected post as governor. "If a man wants to buy an automobile, get married, or run for political office, he will do just that, regardless of advice" became a familiar Clement quote when anyone wondered about his future plans.

He became the nation's youngest governor at age thirty-two and the second-youngest in Tennessee history. By that time he and Cille (a name she preferred) had three sons, nine-year-old Robert (Bob), three-year-old Frank Jr., and James Gary Clement, who was born only twenty-four days after Clement's gubernatorial victory.

In January 1953 the five-member Clement family moved into the Curtiswood Lane governor's residence in South Nashville and began to live the exemplary '50s life on their ten-acre spread.

Frank's son Bob Clement, who went on to become a congressman, remembers: "We had a whole farm out there. We were raising chickens and turkeys, goats, pigs, even a monkey, at the residence. We also had two dogs, both purebred black cocker spaniels. One was Boss and the other was Blackie, named after a favorite TV show, *Boston Blackie*."

Lucille was an impressive singer and piano player, often the main source of musical entertainment in their early days at the official residence. Perhaps it was to please her as well as himself that Clement, the new $12,000-a-year state leader, soon changed the Governor's Mansion into a showcase for musicmakers and music lovers. It would become the most prestigious performance venue in the state capital and, with the governor's support of local performers, helped establish Nashville as the country music capital.

His son Bob describes his father's passionate advocacy of country music. He made "a visit to a congressional hearing in the early days of his administration to defend country music and its artists after a congressman had begun a campaign to denounce the music and stated, 'Country music is obscene literature and ought to be banned!' When the governor was through speaking, so was the uprising."

From that point on, the country music community was at Clement's beck and call. In fact, country artists often performed for him on his campaign stops.

As Clement was lining up his administration and preparing to move to the Governor's Mansion, he had invited his old school friend and confidante James Edwards to his temporary headquarters at the Hermitage Hotel in downtown Nashville for a conversation. The two had grown up as friends in Dickson and had attended Cumberland University together.

Edwards, a former Marine first lieutenant, had spent eighteen months fighting in the Pacific during World War II and was discharged from the service in late 1952. One of Clement's ambitious programs was going to face opposition and he needed someone he could trust. He thought that Edwards might be interested in a challenge.

James Edwards recalls their conversation that day. Clement said, "You remember, back in our school days, we talked about doing something really big, really important? Something to help the state grow? I'm planning a few reforms that some people are not gonna take kindly to, starting with mental health and prison reform. I need your help. I'd like you to be the new warden of the Tennessee State Prison. I've got to make some changes in the system as soon as I can or you can bet your Bible, five to ten years, this state's gonna explode."

"You're going to take on the conservatives, aren't you?" Edwards asked.

"Among other things, but I prefer to think the conservatives are gonna take on God and Frank Clement."

Since Edwards had spent twenty months after the war as a major in a Marine Corps military police battalion, with most of his duty at the Fort Meade, Maryland, prisoner stockade, the job Clement proposed was certainly something Edwards knew how to do. But he had expected a different offer.

He recalls: "I was looking for work after my military service, but nothing like what Frank had in mind. We originally talked about my being adjutant general that day and I told him I'd really like that. He somehow reworked the conversation into the warden direction and kept saying, 'Droopy, you'd be ideal for that job. I really think you ought to give it a try.' Droopy was a nickname I picked up in high school during a basketball game, when I yelled at one of my teammates, 'Shoot the ball, droopy drawers!'

"Anyway, Frank cajoled me into taking a ride out to the prison the next day to look around," Edwards says, "see the conditions and all. I made note of a number of things, including the living quarters for my family and myself, which were quite nice. The salary was about $150 a week and we would have four servants, plus everything was free like the food and rent.

"But I had misgivings about raising two children in that place. I went back to Frank and, with all my mixed feelings, the first thing I thought of I blurted out to him: 'Frank, you need Jesus Christ to do the job at that place. The conditions are intolerable.' Well, he finessed me with, 'I'm the man to make that place tolerable and it would be a prestigious position, having the authority to make meaningful changes and all,' and I said, 'I've got to talk to Evelyn about it.' I called her and she said flippantly, 'I'm right busy now. There anything else you wanna discuss?'"

Persuading his wife wasn't easy, but the next day Edwards told Clement he had decided he'd like to try his hand at overseeing the penitentiary.

On January 16, 1953, James E. Edwards (misidentified in the *Nashville Banner* as an attorney) became the twelfth warden of Tennessee's fifty-five-year-old maximum-security facility. It was the same day as Clement's inauguration.

Edwards, now the youngest warden in the country at age thirty-five, his wife Evelyn (who insisted everybody call her Red), and their two children, Joyce (age five) and Jim (age two), immediately moved into the warden's residence which sat just outside the prison's main gate. Edwards recalls the eerie normality of their daily life: "We had a yard boy, a houseboy, a chef, and a barber . . . and each one of them was in prison for murder. But I trusted them completely and they never let me down. The barber gave me a shave every day with a straight razor." Each morning a school bus pulled up to the main prison gate to pick up Joyce.

It can't ever have seemed completely safe. "We'd been at Old Red [a nickname given the prison because of its bright red, newly tiled roof] just a few days when young Jim disappeared," Edwards recalls. "The guards and I searched frantically and finally found him out on the front lawn. Our yard boy had him riding around on the back of a prison bloodhound. Jim was using the dog's long ears as reins and he was having a ball." (He doesn't report the dog's feelings.)

The houseboy, Paul, was the family favorite. "One day our daughter was playing with her lunch instead of eating, and my wife told her to hurry because the houseboy was waiting to clear the table. 'Come on, Joyce,' she said, 'Paul hasn't got all day.' Paul answered, 'Shucks, ma'am, I got ninety-three more years.'"

Being the warden wasn't going to be easy and Edwards knew it.

"I remember my first day there," Edwards confides. "I walked into my office to find the old warden, Swafford, standing behind my desk. He took the keys, slid 'em across the desk to me, and said, 'Good luck, young fella, you're gonna need it. When do you want me out of your apartment?' I picked up the keys, looked him square in the eyes, and said, 'Yesterday. You knew when I was coming.'" When Edwards took control his charges numbered over thirteen hundred inmates.

During his initial press conference Edwards said, "I appreciate the confidence placed in me by Governor Clement. My main interest will be to do a good job and to see that the prisoners get a fair deal. When prisoners are eligible for parole, I expect to help them in every way I can so that they may return to civic life with a position and work planned in advance for them."

The departing warden, Glen Swafford, didn't think that Edwards could make the institution work. But the inmates were hopeful. Swafford had been a tough and unpopular warden. Edwards recalls:

"Life in a Marine Corps stockade is no Sunday school picnic, but conditions at Old Red were more than I could stomach. My first day there I walked into the filthy mess hall, tasted the slop served for dinner, and assigned the cook to KP."

The next few months of Edwards' transition period became a chess game between cons and correction officers. Some of the inmates confused Edwards' more humane approach with a weakness they intended to exploit. The warden's first problems were parallel: how to reduce the number of convicts under care in the hospital, and what to do about the food dilemma. The food was bad enough that prisoners felt it was making them sick. Edwards changed food suppliers, raised health standards in the kitchen, and improved the portions and variety.

But other reforms were not welcome. The warden changed policy to reduce the role of headbolters by removing their right to hold master keys for the cell tiers. The privilege of holding those keys had been granted by Swafford's administration and was open to flagrant abuse. For a bribe, the inmate turnkey could release prisoners to visit other cells to gamble or socialize. Ed Thurman, for instance, had been known to release the Prisonaires so they could practice in a corner wing of the block. By revoking key control Edwards also reduced the possibility of bribing the guards.

Rumblings throughout the prison got back to Edwards, who anticipated an action by the discontented inmates. His information was that the prisoners would gather in the yard after supper and refuse to go to their cellblocks. Edwards, who had developed as good a grapevine as the inmates had, countered by perching himself in the visitors' gallery, which commanded a clear view of the inner yard and both main wings of the cell blocks.

In the company of several guards, Edwards busied himself by loading and checking riot guns. He told an assistant to pass the word down that they would lock the entrances to the cell wings and, if the men wanted to stay outside, then that was all right with him but they would have to stay outside all night. Within minutes the news had reached the men in the yard. The prospect of staying out all night under the glare of floodlights and the muzzles of the guards' guns, with no shelter from a slow, chilling rain, dissuaded the dissenters.

A few days later a new scheme had been devised. This time the inmates planned to carry stones in their pockets and launch them through the windows opposite their cell tiers just before they entered their cells. Once again, Edwards came up with a creative countermove.

He sent word down that he would open all the windows, turn off the heat, and leave the windows open all night. That prospect had the same chilling effect as the prospect of spending a night outside in the prison yard. When inmates filed into the bitter-cold cellblocks and found the windows open, offering poor targets, they went sheepishly to their cells. Not a rock was thrown.

Johnny Bragg remembers: "The governor once described Warden Edwards as a man who could go out on the back porch and shoot a man, then go out on the front porch and do a dance. If the inmates thought he wasn't tough, they was wrong."

From the prisoners' standpoint, much of the dissatisfaction was residual. It came from the period before Edwards' arrival—what Johnny remembers as "slavin' time."

"It was slavery time back then. If you did anythin' wrong, they beat you with a big strap. Sometimes they killed the inmates."

When Edwards took over he brought along a new deputy warden, John Watt. He summoned Assistant Deputy Neal to his office and stated in no uncertain terms that there would be no beatings in the penitentiary as long as Edwards was warden. And then he took a leather strap that was used for punishment and proceeded to cut it into pieces.

Edwards knew that physical punishment of the prisoners was not going to change things. "Corporal punishment was given for crimes committed inside the prison," he says. "I saw one whipping and got sick. I decided there had to be a better way to maintain discipline and also give the prisoners something to do besides attack each other."

He decided to better morale by improving the environment. "Old Red didn't have much entertainment, so I brought in wrestling matches . . . even lady wrestlers, and the guys loved that. . . . [And] stars from the Grand Ole Opry downtown, and I organized prisoner talent shows. When inmates misbehaved, I got a much better response by barring them from the entertainment than beatings ever accomplished. Even Neal began to come around to mine and the governor's way of thinking after I arrived, and prisoner beatings came to an end."

Edwards slightly exaggerates the extent of the change. Under Warden Swafford, the prison had staged performances by name entertainers, but Edwards significantly increased the number and variety of these events.

Wortham
Music
BMI

Vocal
U-76

JUST WALKIN' IN THE RAIN
(Riley-Bragg)
PRISONAIRES
186
MEMPHIS, TENNESSEE

The Governor Gets a Group

AS WINTER 1953 was coming to an end, the last of the season's hard rains hit the prison just as Johnny was leaving his cell block for the long trudge across the yard to the laundry.

Accompanying him was blockmate Robert Stanley Riley, a twenty-two-year-old habitual housebreaker and thief. He had served three years, from 1946 through 1949, at Brushy Mountain Prison for five cases of larceny, and was sentenced in early 1950 to ten to sixteen years for violating parole by breaking into three more homes to steal clothes and jewelry. Little is known about Riley but his own career was remarkable and he played a key role in the life of Johnny Bragg.

Riley was also a songwriting hopeful, and he and Johnny had struck up a friendship right away. The rain beat down steadily as Johnny looked skyward, part way past the mess hall. "Here we are, just walkin' in the rain. I wonder what the little girls are doin'," he said, almost philosophically, as the twosome strode casually.

"Sounds like a good idea for a song," Riley said as he wiped some rain from his face, picked up the pace, and bellowed back at Johnny, "Well, I don't know what the little girls are doin', but I'm gettin' the hell out of this here rain." With that he raced across the courtyard.

Johnny, oblivious to the downpour, kept his steady pace, talking and singing aloud: "Just walkin' in the rain, gettin' soakin' wet, torturin' my heart, tryin' to forget."

By the time he reached the laundry, Johnny looked ready for the dryer. But he barely even noticed how soaked he was, as he sat down, still singing to himself. "Bob, come'ere. You gotta hear this," he said, and sang almost two full verses to Riley.

Johnny, flushed with enthusiasm, said, "I know this is a hit. I just know it. If you write down the words for me and help me finish it, I'll give you half the song." That was all right by Riley and they proceeded to finish the tune, accompanied by the apropos murmur of the constant rain and the sloshing rhythm of the huge washing machines.

The Sunday morning prayer services held by Chaplain Pickins Johnson always provided an escape for the Prisonaires.

Though the services were held in an auditorium that doubled as a chapel, as the members of the singing group got caught up in the music and emotion of their favorite gospel hymns they could close their eyes and, for a moment or two, they could almost believe they were in their hometown churches, surrounded by their families and friends.

Bob Brassell and the chaplain talked about the beautiful blend and inspired vocals of Johnny and the Prisonaires and Bob suggested to the chaplain that the new warden should hear the boys sing. Two spirituals later, almost as if he had just been given a divine cue, Warden Edwards and several staffers walked into the services. Afterwards the chaplain introduced Edwards to the Prisonaires and told him how the singers had been a blessing and a source of inspiration for many of the other convicts.

Soon after his conversation with the chaplain, Edwards called for the prison records of the group.

He noted that Ed Thurman's father had died when Ed was just a year old and he had been raised by his mother. Thurman had only finished the seventh grade, and his one lifetime mistake was in marked contrast to his deep-rooted religious beliefs. The warden was impressed by Thurman and his Bible-study class.

William Stewart was preoccupied with learning photography and was the prison's movie projectionist.

Marcel Sanders was serving one to five years for involuntary manslaughter. He had stabbed a man in self-defense when the man broke into Marcel's girlfriend's apartment, while Marcel was there, and stabbed the girlfriend and her daughter. Sanders was a second-generation convict; his father had served eight years at the same penitentiary for killing his mother when Marcel was only a year old.

John Drue, who had several prior convictions for auto theft, had finished eighth grade and had spent four years in the army. Edwards gazed long and hard at Drue's picture, trying to remember why he looked so familiar. He finally realized that Drue, considered a minimal escape risk, had been assigned as the warden's chauffeur weeks before.

The warden noted that all had been on good behavior. Feeling more comfortable about his tentative judgment, Edwards summoned the five to his office for an interview. Johnny remembers the occasion vividly: "The warden acted tough, but his message was different than we heard before. He called us 'my fellow inmates' and he said, 'If you do the right thing I'm with you a hundred percent. If you do wrong, I'll be all over ya. We're gonna have a good time, we're gonna change things.' Then he said how our singin' could help the rehabilitation program for the prisoners."

That night the warden dialed the governor's residence to tell Clement about the group. His message was a nice coincidence.

According to sister Anna Belle: "Frank was annoyed with the fact that the state, though providing a budget for food and drinks at the official residence for visiting dignitaries, did not provide for entertainment. Frank told the warden, 'Droopy, I need to find some talent to perform here without a cost to the state.' He [Clement] was always mindful of budgetary concerns."

Warden Edwards, the bearer of timely news, said, "I think I found the answer to your problem," and proceeded to describe his encounter with the Prisonaires.

It seems to have been clear to both Edwards and Clement that the Prisonaires could play an important role as an example of what was possible through prison reform. It's likely that on the day he discovered the group the warden himself was looking for inspiration.

Edwards and the governor had spoken often as to how they might jump-start their prison rehabilitation program by making it visible statewide. Honoring two of his campaign promises, Clement already had pushed through legislation to provide free text books for every grade level extending through high school and had created a mental health department (including the building of modern facilities across the state) separate from the prison system. But prison reform was a tougher task and up to that point they had been stymied for a strategy.

Anna Belle Clement O'Brien continues the story: "Frank went to the prison and saw the group perform in the auditorium. He was overwhelmed by the beauty of their harmony and their sincerity in song."

The Prisonaires didn't know it when they sang those spirituals, but they were auditioning for the governor. Edwards remembers the governor saying he thought they had found their litmus test. "They've even named themselves in a way that leaves no doubt as to who they are and what they represent."

Nevertheless, Clement knew he was taking a risk with public opinion. "If this works," he said, "we're likely to see the best and the worst of our constituency real soon."

Shortly thereafter, James Edwards had the group perform at his home for some guests, both for his own entertainment and also to start spreading the word about his rehabilitation efforts.

Before the new warden had appeared on the scene, no singing group had ever gone beyond the prison walls to sing for any occasion. Now the group began going out with Edwards and guards to sing at churches and civic functions. Wherever Edwards spoke about rehabilitation, he took the five felons along as living, singing proof of the success of his policy.

He realized that the first impressions they made would be lasting ones, and he allowed Thurman and Stewart to begin making suits in the shirt shop for all five Prisonaires. He wanted them to be presentable. Edwards and Clement were going to have to face members of the Ku Klux Klan and other racist Whites, pushing a policy that even many reasonable people would find hard to accept.

Ignorant of the political role developing for them, the group started to become a more cohesive unit. Their harmonies became tighter with each rehearsal, and Johnny began shaping the group's sound into something like that of his idols, the Ink Spots. It was pop/Black music born of a gospel tradition that would soon expand into something even greater—R&B and rock'n'roll.

Johnny's songs of love and loneliness gave the Prisonaires a notable secular style built on their spiritual base. Their effectiveness in performance must have been affected by their commitment to the work. Singing together created solidarity and gave each member of the group the strength to fend off the depression of imprisonment. Making music became their means of psychological survival. Each performance nourished hope. They created an alternative reality, their own free space, right under the guns of the guards.

They seem to have communicated some of that spirit to their audiences. Their slow, sweet, close harmonies heard today have a kind of serenity and precision closer to the music of religious orders.

In the spring of 1953, a news reporter and radio crew came to the penitentiary for a firsthand look at prison life. Joe Calloway of Nashville's WSIX got more than he bargained for.

Warden Edwards wasn't going to miss the opportunity to showcase the prison reform program. The tour was carefully orchestrated to bring Calloway and company into the dining hall just as the Prisonaires let loose with a rousing musical number called "That Chick's

Too Young to Fry," followed by a solemn spiritual. Calloway was fascinated and gleeful that he had found a "rose" growing in such an unlikely place. Surprising Edwards, he asked for permission to have the group sing on WSIX, a White radio station.

The next day the Prisonaires were practicing in the auditorium when Edwards arrived. He spent about half an hour telling the singers of the radio opportunity and the part they would play in convincing the public that rehabilitation programs can work. Edwards' enthusiasm was contagious.

"I remember," Johnny says, "how Warden Edwards taught us to do that stuff with your hands to make the trumpet sound for 'That Chick's Too Young to Fry.'"

A few days later the quintet was driven under armed guard to the WSIX studio in Nashville, and sang their hearts out into an old floor-stand microphone. Their performance was so well received that they were given a regular show. Then, through the efforts of George E. White, public relations man for Black radio station WSOK, they began performing there as well. The sight of five inmates strolling proudly and unshackled out the prison's main gate, in gleaming, matching new suits, was an encouraging spectacle to most inmates. But it also began to provoke envy.

During one of the Prisonaires' impromptu performances at WSIX, someone turned on a tape machine and the group heard what they sounded like for the first time. Though Ed Thurman was inexplicably absent from that taping, they now had recorded versions of "Just Walkin' in the Rain," "That Chick's Too Young to Fry," a Robert Riley song "Baby Please," and a tune called "Dreamin' of You."

Apparently short of tape, the station's engineer had recorded the Prisonaires' songs over a show called *Youth on Parade*, starring a newcomer named Pat Boone. That was probably one of the few times that a Black act ever came out on top of Boone, who would become known for recording Black artists' new songs and beating them to the pop charts with his own pasteurized versions.

That afternoon Edwards met Johnny in the yard and told him that the governor would like the group to sing at the Mansion the next evening. They would leave at four o'clock and would be driven in the warden's car. Johnny wasn't sure that the time was yet right.

"I would not send you if you were not ready. Besides, the governor is on your side. . . . You know, it's *not* the Grand Ole Opry. . . . Relax."

"Maybe one day it will be," Johnny thought.

The group was supposed to be driven from the prison accompanied by a guard and a highway patrol escort. But on their first trip to the Governor's Mansion, as they approached the car, they noticed that Red Edwards, the warden's petite wife, was behind the wheel. "Get in. We're already late," she ordered. William stammered, "Ah, yes'm, Mrs. Warden."

The car pulled out with a screech of tires, which was a mere prelude to Red's daredevil approach to driving. "Bet you're wondering where Officer Martin is," she said as she wheeled the car around a curve. "Yes, Ma'am," Johnny answered in his most polite tone. "Damned if I know, but someone had to get you to the governor's," Red replied in feigned annoyance. But she wasn't able to hide her own enthusiasm. An invitation to one of the governor's parties was the hottest ticket in town.

As the car turned up the circular driveway, the Mansion itself—fifteen thousand square feet—loomed large over the grounds. Bought by the state in 1948 from insurance magnate William Ridley Wills for $120,350, the 1929 Georgian brick estate boasted twenty-two rooms covering two floors. It was maintained by a staff of sixteen people who were mostly trustees from the prison. "Farhills," as it was known prior to political occupation, initially became the state's first-family residence in 1949 when Governor Gordon Browning moved in.

The group exited the car at the front entrance to the Mansion and a servant drove the car away. Inside the impressive white pillars on the porch, Red waited with the singers at the heavy wooden doors with the handcrafted brass peacock knockers.

"Are you sure we're s'posed to be comin' in the front door, ma'am?" Ed asked. At that time, Blacks rarely entered the buildings of Whites by the front door.

Red Edwards waved them in impatiently and led them through the majestic entranceway. The checkerboard floor, like those in English manor homes, was done in foot-square, white marble from Georgia and black marble from Belgium. To the right stood an elegant curved staircase with pickled wrought-iron railings. Used primarily for state functions, the first floor included a large formal drawing room. Among the other main rooms, three steps down from the drawing room was a sun room, along with a state dining room, a family dining room, the kitchen, and a library the governor used as his home office.

Mrs. Edwards led the group up the grand staircase to the second floor, which included five bedrooms and six baths, and a sitting room that doubled as a room for entertainment.

A grand piano sat at one end of the room near the large French windows and doors that led out to a balcony. On the opposite side of the chamber were chairs and sofas for about twenty, arranged in a semicircle around the piano. Mrs. Edwards motioned for one of the governor's aides to come over and told him these men were the Prisonaires, vocal performers for that evening's entertainment.

Red departed swiftly down the hall and the aide smiled widely until she was out of sight. Then he was transformed.

Johnny recalls the aide saying to them, "I don't know how you niggers wrangled your way up here but you even think of somethin' foolish and the troopers have orders to shoot to kill!" He told them they were confined to the room. "Governor says you can leave by the front door when your driver tells you to. Me, I'd just as soon flush you down the toilet." When the governor appeared the climate changed again. "I was just going over the evening's procedures with the prisoners," the aide said.

"They are not prisoners here, they're singers," the governor told him. He proceeded to make sure he had the singers' names correct. "Now let's see if I've got this right. You're William, the guitarist; you're Edward, Marcel, Junior, and you're Johnny, the lead singer."

The members looked at each other in astonishment that the governor would know their names, let alone who was who. Clement's photographic memory, surely a God-given gift for a politician, was as valuable a persuasive tool with the less-privileged as it was with the privileged.

"We're right pleased to be here, Governor," Johnny mumbled.

The governor told the group to sing a mix of spirituals and popular songs for his guests. He said they were going to help turn a lot of ornery politicians and bigots into friends, if they sang the way they had at prison. He tried to put the convicts at ease and told them not to let the big shots make them nervous. Clement also told the group that since he had that "bull-headed Texas senator, Lyndon Johnson" visiting, he

wanted them to sing something especially God-fearing and look Johnson straight in the eye. "He'll think God's looking over his shoulder."

From the very beginning, Clement made it clear that this was not
just a one-shot gig but an opportunity. Johnny wasn't afraid to ask,
"Governor, sir, do you do this often, I mean like, every couple a months?
We'll be happy to work here as often as you need us."

Clement told Johnny he staged such events three or four times a
week. He hoped they were ready to entertain when needed. As he was
leaving the room he turned back to Johnny with a smile and said,
"Actually, that's a fair assessment of the situation. We need each
other. Don't ever forget that."

The affair that evening was small but elegant. After supper about fifteen well-dressed guests assembled in the sitting room. The governor,
Cuban cigar in hand, stood next to the baby grand piano and asked
his guests to take their seats.

He told his audience that the evening's entertainment was not
just a tremendous singing group, which he was proud to say he discovered, but were proof positive of the immediate success of his
rehabilitation program. "That's right, each of these well-dressed men
are inmates at our state penitentiary."

Clement was a young man who had a young man's zeal for his
own bright ideas. He loved the shock value of what he was doing.
He told his guests that these inmates had been performing at church
services and civic functions all over Nashville.

Johnny remembers that Clement concluded, "I know they're
good because Senator Gore over there has tried to borrow 'em from
me several times." (Gore had also heard the Prisonaires sing while
visiting a church service.)

And Johnny remembers Senator Johnson quipping, in his slow Texas drawl, "Ah, Frank, if this goes well for ya, perhaps ya'll go into the booking business."

The group opened with a spirited gospel number and, as they'd been told to do, Johnny stared right at Senator Johnson as he was singing the "God-fearin'" parts. He remembers that he could see the senator's discomfort.

The quintet performed a number of songs and then moved to the kitchen, where they were given supper while the obligatory speeches went on. They then came out for a second, lengthy performance of gospel and pop songs.

After their finale the Prisonaires were surprised to be approached by guests. These five Black men, most of them condemned to long sentences, had awakened in cells that morning, had eaten in the prison dining halls, and now they were *mingling*. The governor didn't discourage it. The Mansion guards were apparently under orders to be discreet and were barely in evidence. At about 11:00 P.M. the group was inconspicuously escorted out via the same front-door route.

"I couldn't believe we was there," Johnny says. "I never knew people lived so good and we was part of it, least for a while." The Prisonaires, like Cinderella, returned to the prison, where they replaced their suits with their usual prison garb and turned back into convicts.

The evening had been a huge success and Clement moved to take advantage of it. He legitimized the group by inviting Johnny and company to perform regularly at the executive residence. He reasoned that there was no better way to put forward his prison reform policy than to have the very lawmakers, high society opposition, and "fence-sitters" who regularly visited the Governor's Mansion be persuaded by the music and by the example of the group. It was as if they were being entertained into submission. It was a bold move.

The Prisonaires could be not only a great example of how prison reform works but, in fact, also a test of the theory that criminals could be rehabilitated. From the beginning, Clement knew that his own political fortunes were, in part, going to be affected by these five Black men.

News of what a Southern friend tells me the Klan called the "niggers' night" at the Mansion added to the controversy already burning over school desegregation.

Brown v. the Board of Education had been argued before the Supreme Court in December 1952. No decision had been handed down. The Court had heard arguments again on the issue in December of the following year. They deliberated for six months before handing down their decision in May 1954.

For Southern politicians, any conflict over racial issues was a no-win affair. In 1953 Tennessee, Whites and Blacks not only were forbidden to attend the same schools but housing was also segregated, as was everything from hospitals and theaters to barber shops. Even insane asylums and homes for the blind were segregated.

But many astute political figures knew desegregation was coming inevitably. The new, post-war, industrial economy couldn't function with old agrarian models. Nor could the country tolerate a permanent underclass. This was the political and moral reality that Frank Clement stepped into as the state's new governor.

Within weeks of the Prisonaires' initial WSIX and WSOK performances, music publisher Red Wortham came to the prison seeking a hillbilly songwriter he'd heard about (possibly Clarence "Two Flats" McKeel), in hopes of finding new music to publish. While there, he was also asked to listen to the Prisonaires. Wortham said he was more a judge of music than of talent, but agreed to listen. Impressed more than he thought possible, Wortham took a tape back with him (presumably of the WSIX recordings) and played it for his cousin Jim Bulleit. Jim owned his own Bullet record label but, more important, was a part owner in Memphis Recording Service and its new label, Sun Records.

Sam Phillips was co-owner of Sun, whose biggest success until that time was a song taped at Memphis Recording but owned by Chess Records, entitled "Rocket 88" and credited on the label as being by Jackie Brenston. The record was actually made by Ike Turner and his Kings of Rhythm, featuring Brenston on sax and lead vocal. "Rocket 88" reached number one on the national R&B charts in 1951 and has been identified by some as the first rock'n'roll record.

The youngest of eight children, Sam Phillips was from Florence, Alabama. He had played sousaphone at Coffee High School, but his musical ambitions were nil. Sam's original intent in life was to be a criminal defense lawyer. He was a teetotaler, a young man of principles, concerned about justice and equality. His dream of a legal career had disappeared with the death of his father.

Facing the responsibility of caring for his mother and aunt, he went to work. His older brother, Jud, had a job at radio WLAY in Muscle Shoals, Alabama, and so Sam joined him, finally winding up in Memphis with WREC in 1945 as an announcer and maintenance engineer. He opened his own recording studio in January 1950, taking his concern for justice in a musical direction with a plan to provide opportunities for Black artists to record. Making ends meet by taping everything he could drag in the door, his business card read "We Record Anything—Anywhere—Anytime." Sam had been on the lookout for something new when Jim called.

Bulleit believed the Prisonaires were tremendous talents and recommended that Phillips sign them. Sam was skeptical, but heard the tape and thought they were terrific. When he heard where the group was residing he probably wondered if he'd have to break them out of prison to record them. Bulleit told Sam that the new warden was high on rehabilitation and that this would be good publicity for the warden's prison reform program.

So Jim drove back to Nashville to see Warden Edwards. The warden's response was not what he'd hoped for. Edwards, though sympathetic, was dubious. At first he missed the point of Bulleit's proposal, stating only that the inmates wouldn't be able to keep most of what they earned. Discouraged, Bulleit left. Soon after, however, he decided to take his case to the governor.

By that time Edwards had spoken with Clement. Clement was in favor of anything in the world that would not only help to rehabilitate the five singers, but would also serve as an inspiration to other inmates and create good will outside the prison. A successful career for the Prisonaires could only make him and Edwards look good. With the governor's permission, Bulleit set about making arrangements with Sam Phillips for a studio date.

When the warden called them to his office, Johnny could only assume it was for another civic function. When he heard the words "recording session" and "long drive," his mind shut out everything else. As the warden went on about trust, responsibility, and something like "don't be nervous," Johnny just kept thinking to himself, "Thank you, Lord, for giving us this opportunity."

Wortham
Music
BMI

Vocal
U-75

BABY PLEASE
(Riley)
PRISONAIRES
186
MEMPHIS, TENNESSEE

The "Just Walkin'" Session

BY 7:30 A.M. on the Monday morning of June 1, 1953, Jim Bulleit parked outside the main gate of the Tennessee penitentiary in a white van, awaiting his traveling companions—a guard, a trustee, and five dapper-looking convict singers.

Memphis is about 190 miles west-southwest of Nashville and the old, two-lane, blacktop Route 70 was a bumpy, uncomfortable ride. But for Johnny it was like a highway to heaven. He'd never known of any inmate having the chance he was getting. The strangeness of his situation became clearer as they drove through a landscape that had been transformed while he was in prison. Johnny Bragg was deeply out of touch. At one point he looked out the rear window of the van and remarked, "Gee, look at that funny cemetery."

"That ain't no cemetery, John," Marcel told him, "that's one of them there drive-in movies."

The ten years, almost to the day, of Johnny's separation from society came home with a thud as he realized how much he had missed in the outside world. Johnny sat silently for the rest of the long ride.

The Prisonaires arrived in Memphis after 10:00 A.M. and entered the Sun Records storefront studio at 706 Union Avenue, a former auto repair shop. There Jim Bulleit introduced the singers to thirty-year-old Sam Phillips—handsome, dark-haired, and imposing—and Bulleit also introduced them to Jud Phillips.

Sam shook the hand of each member of the group with enthusiasm. He'd been recording Black artists for two years but was still looking for a big hit for his young record label.

The trustee and guard then went next door for coffee, and Sam sent the group to the studio as he, Jud, and Jim went into the recording booth. Sam was concerned about whether the group was rehearsed, but Jim told him to relax and give them a chance. From the booth Sam hit the talk button to ask the group what the first song would be. While still trying to figure out what part of the floor-stand microphone to sing into, Johnny told them they wanted to record his song "Just Walkin' in the Rain."

The Prisonaires went to work finding the right sound for "Just Walkin'" while Sam maneuvered the dials to get a sound level. Jud and Jim settled into their chairs as the group got down to business. What had flowed effortlessly on the state penitentiary stage was captured in

all its inadequacy by the studio recorder. Sam told the group their harmony sounded fine, but was critical of Johnny's vocals: "Your diction's
off. On 'torturing' you're going 'torturin,'" and it's 'just' not 'jist' and
'changed' not 'chaged.' Got that? Let's try it again."

The group tried it over and over as the clock ticked into the
afternoon but Johnny just couldn't seem to get it right. They repeated,
recorded, rehearsed, and repeated again, but still they hadn't gotten
anything useable. Finally, according to Johnny, Sam left the booth
and motioned the group into the reception area to tell them he didn't
think this was going to work. Sam said he thought they should return
to Nashville.

As Johnny tells it, there appeared suddenly, from a corner of the
waiting room, a tall, dust-covered White teenager with torn jeans and
a sheepish smile. Sam said to no one in particular, "This guy's been
trying to slip in here for two weeks." The young man, reportedly,
wanted to record a song as a present for his mother. (It later became
known that he had been too shy to admit he wanted to record for
himself, so he made up the story about his mother—whose birthday
was actually in April.)

Johnny's description of the way his predicament was resolved is
extraordinary. "I could hit the notes, but my diction was bad, and
this guy came outta nowhere," Johnny remembers. "I can help you
with those words," the kid said. But Sam wasn't listening as he
grabbed the kid by the shirt and walked him to the door, telling him,
"I'm gonna put your ass in jail. We got all these nigger convicts down
here, something happens, they'll call us down."

Johnny interceded. "Please, Mr. Phillips, give 'im a chance. We
can't get 'Just Walkin' in the Rain' to *sound like* 'Just Walkin' in the
Rain.' Let 'im try."

Sam apparently thought it over and decided to take a break for lunch. With that the group settled into the waiting room, where sandwiches were brought from next door, while Sam went to his usual booth at Miss Taylor's for a bite, leaving Johnny, the teenager, and Sam's brother, Jud.

For almost an hour the kid and the convict sat in the studio, door closed, equipment off, while the lesson proceeded and the two struggled through their rehearsal. Johnny recalls: "We got lucky. He didn't know what he was doin' and I didn't know what I was doin', but I had the voice though, and he was a White guy singin' Black music himself."

When Sam and Jim returned and asked Johnny if he was ready, Johnny answered, "I hope so, Mr. Phillips. Is it okay if he stays in here and just kinda mouths the words for me?" Sam apparently nodded approval and hit the talk button, "'Just Walkin' in the Rain,' take one."

The group started singing. And kept singing. Everything had come together. Johnny's vocal was vibrant, smooth, and clear. The group was harmonious and tight. William's easygoing acoustic guitar accompaniment kept the team's timing together and augmented without overshadowing their blend. When the quintet finished the take, Sam walked into the studio and told them it was fine. He had to admit Johnny had somehow made it work.

Then, according to Johnny, Sam turned to the White teenager and asked his name. The young man spoke respectfully and introduced himself as Elvis Presley.

Sam went back in the booth while Johnny stood in the studio doorway. "Thanks for your help, Presley."

"It wasn't nothin'," the high schooler, just a few days from his graduation, said smiling softly.

"No, it was somethin'. Maybe we helped each other," the convict replied.

"I hope so. See ya, Johnny."

Johnny was more than grateful. The kid had saved his shot at success.

Later Johnny came to believe that the favor had cut two ways. "Sam Phillips got happy and that's how Presley got his break. Sam told Presley he done such a good job with me, if he would come back, he would let him cut a record [presumably a demo]." Though the moment is vivid in Johnny's mind, no one at Sun acknowledged an offer to Presley. That offer would come later.

According to Johnny, this was the first of several meetings, and of the many times that Johnny would call him simply "Presley." For his own subconscious reasons he never would use Elvis's first name to the future rock king's face.

Sometime during that summer, Elvis did the demos he'd wanted to do. Interestingly, Johnny was not the only Ink Spots–inspired singer of his day. One of the first two demos Elvis recorded was the Ink Spots' 1941 hit "That's When Your Heartaches Begin."

It might be tempting to see these stories as apocryphal, as Johnny Bragg's attempt to re-create mythically a sense of his own place in the new interracial culture. But in fact most of Bragg's stories can be documented from other sources—which at least suggests the probability that they are true.

Jud Phillips remembered the session and reaffirmed the story about Elvis, including in a September 1977 *Nashville Banner* article in which he said: "We had strict orders not to let anybody in because we had all those prisoners down here. I remember that Elvis was coming in and out of the studio at that time and I remember Elvis being there that day. It wasn't any earth-shaking event at the time, of course, but I think Elvis was allowed in the studio with Bragg."

The Prisonaires got back to work in the studio with a rundown of the Robert Riley song "Baby Please." "Please" was a blues tune that took on smooth harmony and pop overtones, with Stewart's gentle guitar work. It was, however, a style that held little interest for Sam, who preferred the raw animalism of straight blues.

Hoping to spice up the group's syrupy sound, he called over to a local bottler, Don Canale, whose houseboy, Joe Hill Lewis, played a mean, unsophisticated blues guitar. Lewis added his touches, making "Baby Please" into a bouncy rhythm ballad. Ed Thurman's floating falsetto created a sound that today seems to herald northern doo-wop records, still two years in the future.

Between takes Lewis, in a classic understatement, said to Johnny: "You guys are good, but you have to remember you've got to stick together." Johnny, with *only* 584 years of servitude left, looked at him matter-of-factly and deadpanned, "Not much chance of us *not* stickin' together."

By the time "Baby Please" was put to bed and the group had run down several long-since-forgotten tunes that Sam Phillips decided not to tape, it was 8:30 at night. Sam's first instinct was for "Baby Please" to be the A side (the side of the record to be promoted to radio stations; also called the pick hit or top side).

But as they sat in the darkness of the van on their way back to the penitentiary, the Prisonaires—as united in their opinion as they were in their harmonies—were sure that "Just Walkin' in the Rain" was the A side.

RECORD NO.
9-30972
107,999+
(2:30)

Vocal With
Chorus And
Instrumental
Accompaniment

EVERYTHING'S ALRIGHT
(Johnny Bragg)
JOHNNY BRAGG

Hard Time Hit-Makers

ON JULY 15, 1953, the *Memphis Commercial Appeal* reported the unusual events of the preceding month. The newspaper account of the convicts was a novel story at the very least, but it also indicated the start of something much bigger.

Governor Clement was prepared for the moment and was quoted that day as having said, "The Prisonaires represent the hopes of tomorrow rather than the mistakes of yesterday. They are a part of our program of rehabilitation and their musical message is for the people everywhere and not merely for themselves."

Clement and Edwards intended to do more than offer eloquent prose for the papers. One morning shortly after the session, Warden

Edwards told the Prisonaires that they were going to perform on radio station WSM that coming weekend. WSM was the home of the Grand Ole Opry, a Southern institution since 1926. Edwards had for some time been bringing Opry entertainers to perform for the inmates. Now, he thought, he had a chance to turn things around.

That Friday evening, wearing their summer suits, the Prisonaires approached the Ryman Auditorium that housed WSM. They piled out of the prison van, past their highway patrol escort, and entered the auditorium through a side door. Like Edwards, they thought they were making a breakthrough.

The hope was premature; the racial realities of the South would not be easily changed even at the behest of the warden and the governor. The Prisonaires were let in the door but wound up performing on *The Friday Night Frolics,* a prelude show without the Opry's prestige, instead of on the Grand Ole Opry's showcase. The quintet appeared early in the evening and was ushered back to their van and sent on their way before they could hear anyone else perform.

Whenever the group returned from performing outside the walls, other convicts checked by to ask what it was like to feel free and appreciated, if only for the moment. This time the news was not good.

In the middle of June the Nashville Exchange Club hosted a luncheon at the Hermitage Hotel featuring Warden Edwards as guest speaker. The *Nashville Banner* reported the event under the headline "Warden Edwards Cites Prison Improvements."

Edwards told the club, "Tennessee is renewing efforts to improve conditions in penal institutions in a more determined manner, despite the fact the state is fifty years behind modern prison plans."

The warden deplored some conditions in the prison, but said an employment bureau had been created to find work for inmates when their sentences were completed. "They need a job when they leave the prison, but they also need more than that," he said as he explained that the state currently gave a man only a bus ticket and $1.50 to get to his home. "Officials are exerting every effort to give the inmates a specific daily job. On the 3,600-acre penitentiary farm," he said, "prisoners have planted five hundred acres of corn, six hundred acres of small grain, and attended four hundred head of beef cattle." With reference to rehabilitation, the warden said, "the administration of Governor Frank Clement has inaugurated a policy of treating the prisoners as individuals, and is making every effort to correct various problems of the inmates." He said, "The state is feeding the prisoners more adequately, and is providing in addition to work, a recreation and entertainment program, which has proven highly successful."

The newspaper story added: "Through the courtesy of Warden Edwards, Exchange Club members were entertained by the prisoner quintet. Their group of Negro singers, which has already recorded several songs, was loudly applauded by the civic club members."

Slowly but surely, Johnny Bragg was becoming a minor pop celebrity. But unlike other young men becoming successful in the mid-century, he could not leave his past behind. He could not escape the fact that he was Black in a time when Blacks had very few chances to succeed. He surely could not escape the consequences of his alleged crimes. Nor could he escape the darker sides of American culture. This was an era in which execution of criminals was commonplace, as it is beginning to be again today.

On Thursday, June 19, 1953, the Rosenbergs, convicted of passing H-bomb secrets to the Soviets, went to the electric chair. Johnny Bragg had firsthand experience of such things. He sometimes wondered how his everyday experiences could bridge such extremes. He alternated between the exhilaration of performing before enthusiastic audiences, and a daily life bounded by steel mesh, bars, heavy concrete walls, and death: he was electrifying audiences with his performances at night, and dealing with the degradation of those electrocuted during the day. He believes—and who can doubt it?—that his stubbornness, his determination to accomplish something with his life, and, most of all, his unerring faith in God made him numb during those frightening and horrible times. Even other inmates found the incongruities of Johnny's life hard to reconcile.

At the time of the Rosenberg execution, Johnny assisted at one closer to his domain. He was working again with Ray Bryant, lifting a tall Black man off the electric chair.

"What'd it feel like?" Ray asked as they worked.

"What'd what feel like?" asked Johnny.

"Recording a song. Y' know, like a radio star," Ray said.

"Scary . . . but real nice, like singin' at the governor's place. All those people listenin' and clappin'. It's another life out there."

"You gonna keep doin' it?" Ray asked as they dropped the body on a gurney.

"Long as I can," Johnny said.

"You a convict, boy, for life! How can you go so high and come back to somethin' so low all the time?" Ray asked.

Johnny remembers that he didn't answer. He just turned and stared at the electric chair as if death were the alternative.

1953. The original sheet music for the Prisonaires' hit, "Just Walkin' in the Rain." The highly sought-after collectible is one of the rarest pieces of R&B sheet music in existence, commanding a price in excess of $600. COURTESY OF GENE AUTRY MUSIC GROUP ©1953, RENEWED GOLDEN WEST MELODIES

TOP: 1953. The members of the quintet, wearing suits they made themselves within the prison walls, leaving the Tennessee State Prison on their way to one of countless performances. COURTESY OF SHOWTIME ARCHIVES (TORONTO)

BOTTOM: 1953. The group's first performance at Nashville's Black radio station WSOK was so well-received that they were given a regular weekly spot. COURTESY OF SHOWTIME ARCHIVES (TORONTO)

TOP: 1953. The group never failed to draw a crowd of curious convicts and guards with tales of their performances on the outside. COURTESY OF SHOWTIME ARCHIVES (TORONTO)

BOTTOM: 1953. STANDING, L–R: Drue, Sanders, Stewart, Thurman; SEATED: Bragg, Bob Clement, James Proctor (co-writer of "A Prisoner's Prayer" and member of the Tennessee Bureau of Criminal Identification). Photo taken at the Governor's Mansion. COURTESY OF SHOWTIME ARCHIVES (TORONTO)

THE CASH BOX
The Nation's
Rhythm & Blues
TOP TEN

1 CRYING IN THE
CHAPEL
The Orioles
(Jubilee 5122)

2 GOOD LOVIN'
The Clovers
(Atlantic 1000)

3 THE CLOCK
Johnny Ace
(Duke 112)

4 SHAKE A HAND
Faye Adams & Joe Morris
(Herald 416)

5 PLEASE DON'T
LEAVE ME
Fats Domino
(Imperial 5240)

6 TOO MUCH LOVIN'
The "5" Royales
(Apollo 448)

7 PLEASE LOVE ME
B. B. King
(R.P.M. 386)

8 GET IT
The Royals
(Federal 12133)

9 DON'T DECEIVE ME
Chuck Willis
(Okeh 6985)

10 JUST WALKIN'
IN THE RAIN
Prisonaires
(Sun 186)

FAR LEFT: SEPTEMBER 5, 1953. "Just Walkin' in the Rain" reaches the national R&B Top Ten, becoming Sun Records' first and only vocal-group hit. COURTESY OF *CASH BOX* MAGAZINE

TOP: 1959. Backstage after a show with Ray Charles. COURTESY OF SHOWTIME ARCHIVES (TORONTO)

CENTER: 1959. Bobby Day, Johnny Bragg, and LaVern Baker. COURTESY OF JHB ARCHIVES

LEFT: 1959. Johnnie Ray, who took the Prisonaires' R&B hit and made it into an international two-million seller. COURTESY OF BROADCAST MUSIC, INC.

TOP: 1959. Johnny Bragg made his one and only performance appearance at the Grand Ole Opry. L–R: (unknown), Dale Potter, Alfred Brooks, Hubbard Brown, Buddy Emmons, Johnny Bragg, Leon Rhodes, Del Wood, Little Jimmy Dickens, (unknown), L. B. McCollough, Willy Wilson, (BENDING OVER) Robert Riley, Henry "Dishrag" Jones. COURTESY OF SHOWTIME ARCHIVES (TORONTO)

BOTTOM LEFT: 1966. The Prisonaires' last incarnation at a performance in Jackson, Tennessee. L–R: Johnny Bragg, Acie Horton, Alfred Brooks, Sullivan Hayes, Marcel Sanders, and James Doyle. COURTESY OF JACKSON SUN ARCHIVES

BOTTOM RIGHT: 1959. Bragg in his high-life, trademark tuxedo and bowler hat—the same outfit he was wearing the day he was arrested for "breach of the peace" and thrown into a lineup with four convicts dressed in jailstripes. COURTESY OF JHB ARCHIVES

TOP: 1959. The Marigolds: Henry "Dishrag" Jones (SEATED AT PIANO), Hal Hebb, Johnny Bragg, John Drue Jr., L. B. McCollough, Alfred Brooks, Willy Wilson. COURTESY OF JHB ARCHIVES

BOTTOM: 1955. A rehearsal at the prison auditorium with several of the Marigolds and members of the prison orchestra. FAR RIGHT, STANDING is Johnny Bragg. COURTESY OF JHB ARCHIVES

TOP: 1964. The only known photo of the latter-day Prisonaires with their only White member, Clarence "Two Flats" McKeel. L–R: McKeel, Johnny Bragg, Acie Horton, Sullivan Hayes, and James Doyle. COURTESY OF JHB ARCHIVES

BOTTOM: 1953. The original group performing at an upscale White hotel. During that first year on their own tour circuit, they left the prison more than 200 times. L–R: John Drue Jr., Johnny Bragg, Ed Thurman, William Stewart, and Marcel Sanders. COURTESY OF JHB ARCHIVES

FOLLOWING PAGE: 1959. Publicity photo used by Johnny Bragg during his first year as a free man. COURTESY OF JHB ARCHIVES

Each day that passed since the session at Sun Records created both anxiety and excitement about the pending release of the first record. In the days of two-track audio recording, and vinyl seven-inch singles, it was not unusual for a song to be recorded on a Monday, pressed on a Tuesday, on the radio Wednesday, and in the stores on Thursday.

The Prisonaires' first single moved more slowly. Its issue date was July 8, five weeks after the act's recording session. It took five weeks more, until August 15, before *Billboard* reviewed the record. But when it did, the record got a solid recommendation in—surprisingly—the pop category, a section with a larger market potential than the R&B section.

The *Billboard* review chose "Baby Please" as the pick-hit side, giving it a rating of 65, while stating that the group of convicts who had formed a singing group sounded "pretty good on this ballad effort." "Just Walkin' in the Rain" also got a 65, and the review said, in part, that the members of the group "deliver it in a warmly blended effort for some more good listening."

(*Billboard* and *Cash Box* [which ceased operation in 1994] magazines were weekly music-industry bibles, recording all relevant activities within the industry. Reviews were perused by record stores and radio disc jockeys to decide, along with the record's chart information, what new records to stock and play. The score of 65 reflected *Billboard*'s ranking system: 50–59 Limited; 60–69 Satisfactory; 70–79 Good; 80–89 Excellent; 90–100 Tops.)

Other records reviewed that day that would become part of pop and R&B music's legacy included the Four Vagabonds' "P.S. I Love You," the Flamingos' "That's My Desire," Joe Turner's "Honey Hush," and "All I Do Is Dream of You," the sixteenth chart record for Johnnie

Ray, an artist who would have a tremendous effect on Johnny Bragg's life. Coincidentally, the Ink Spots' new single that same day was "Don't Mind the Rain," a song that sounded as if it were an answer record to the Prisonaires' "Just Walkin' in the Rain" (along with a relatable title for the inmates, the B-side ballad "Do You Know What It Means to Be Lonely?").

As was expected, WSOK, one of the two radio stations that gave the group their start, broadcast the record first—that evening in fact. Johnny remembers the first-time excitement as if it were a first dollar earned or a first sexual conquest: "We was comin' in from dinner. Some of the guys were already in their cells. I passed Ed's headbolter desk where a radio was playin'. I gets within earshot and I keep movin' closer to a familiar sound. The radio's playin' 'Just Walkin.' Ed, he walked in behind me and sat at his desk. I said, 'Ed, you hear that? That's us!' Ed, he said, 'Yeah, it is. Sounds all right.'

"Then I yelled up to the second floor to Marcel, 'Marcel, you hear it?' Voices started comin' outta different cells all over the place. Marcel, he got real excited. 'I hear it, I hear it!' he kept yelling. The guards, they were looking us up and down, but they let it go."

By the time Junior Drue joined in, applause, whistles, and cheers came from all over the Negro block, totally drowning out the music from the old tube radio.

Then William Stewart chimed in at full volume from the third level, "Yeah, if that don't beat all. We're on our way." Thurman, into his thirteenth year of confinement, simply said, "Yeah, but where?"

Radio stations up and down the East Coast and throughout the South began playing the Prisonaires' song, and Sam Phillips was astonished to see thousands of record orders roll in. Newspapers and magazines throughout the country picked up the story of "the cons who could," and included in most was a comment on the rehabilitation policies of Clement and Edwards.

Two days after the record's release, the *Nashville Tennessean* featured an article titled "Stock car races tonight, help kids to play," and stated, in part:

> . . . stars of the musical portion of the night's events will be Big Jeff and his Radio Playboys, popular hillbilly entertainers, and the Prisonaires Negro vocal group, two groups with widely varying styles. Big Jeff has been hillbilly emcee of WLAC's 'Saturday Frolic' for thirteen years, and his Radio Playboys have toured the south playing in high school auditoriums and theaters. The Prisonaires, inmates at Tennessee State Prison here, have become increasingly popular in this area as a result of recent appearances on WSM-TV, radio stations WSM, WSIX, and WSOK. Their first platter, 'Just Walkin' in the Rain' and 'Baby Please,' was released only two days ago by Sun Records.

The article featured a photo of the group that would become their best-known and the one most widely used in future newspaper and magazine articles. It showed a seated Johnny Bragg with John Drue, William Stewart, Marcel Sanders, and Ed Thurman standing over and to the right of Johnny, each attired in a white sports jacket and shirt, black bow tie, and dark trousers.

A week later the newspaper took up the story in greater depth, with the headline "Prison Vocal Group Hits Jackpot Walkin' in the Rain." It said:

A Nashville Negro's vocal group may have a money-making record "hit" on the market, but it will be a long time before it pays off for them. They're all in prison. The quintet, who calls themselves the Prisonaires, had to cut their record, "Just Walkin' in the Rain," in Memphis, under armed guards. All are inmates of the State Prison here. Nothing but samples of the groups first record have been put on the market yet, and they've only been out a week, but already more than 20,000 orders have piled up.

The article went on to note, with one inaccuracy regarding the song's composers:

The quintet was organized in prison and none of the members had much experience before getting together behind bars. The composer of the "could be" hit is also a Negro prisoner here, Robert S. Riley. Known as a prolific songwriter, this will be his first hit if it clicks. Jim Bulleit, partner in the Memphis Recording Services who also had a hand in publishing Francis Craig's famous "Near You" several years ago, says "Just Walkin'" is setting a better early pace than did Craig's big hit.

Unfortunately for the Prisonaires, they won't be able to get their hands on any money earned by the record. It will be put in the prison bank for them. However, twenty percent of it at their suggestion, will go to the inmates' fund to help fellow convicts. The tune is a sad ditty about a guy "Trying to forget, Just walkin' in the rain," but ironically, neither the singers nor the composer have the privilege they sing about. All have inside jobs at the prison.

The twenty-percent fund was the idea of Thurman and Bragg. From their long tenure in the prison, Ed and Johnny, more than the others, had a keen sense of the flip side of their popularity: other inmates envied them.

Johnny remembers: "You had a lot of guards back there that didn't like the idea of what we were doin'. . . . The most important thing was the inmates . . . see, if the inmates didn't like it, you couldn't make it. It was up to the inmates, not the governor, because if they didn't like it, they'd kill you, so the inmates were behind us a hundred percent. The White boys and the Black boys, that's the way it was. And it was strictly a Black group!"

Over the coming years, tension would grow among the prison population between the privileged performers and those convicts who resented their success.

For now, however, most of the inmates seemed to be rooting for the Prisonaires, finding in them some hope for their own futures. New vocal groups began springing up all over the yard. One act, a short-lived foursome called the Ebonaires, was even beginning to make some progress beyond the walls for an occasional church event, but no act had the quality and momentum of the Prisonaires.

Sam Phillips was delighted over his first venture with a vocal group. He hadn't expected to love the convicts, but record sales were going through the roof. One newspaper reported that the Prisonaires were the first inmates to have a successful career while in prison, and called them "The Hard Time Hit-Makers."

Sam knew the record was a good one, and though he had put out "Baby Please" as the A side, he was just as happy to have all the disc jockeys flipping it to "Just Walkin' in the Rain." Sam began thinking about putting out the next single with prison stripes on the label, and Jud Phillips thought that a better idea might be to take their equipment to Nashville and record the group right there in the prison.

On July 28, Jud Phillips motored up to Nashville to meet with the group while he was on a promotion tour for their record. Jim Bulleit joined him and they met with the singers in the auditorium. Jud Phillips discovered that his artists were receiving fan mail. He wrote Sam that the boys were getting ten to twenty-five letters a day from all over the country. "They make me think of a bunch of baby birds. They're fine boys, all of them. I get great joy out of helping people like that—I know you do too." During the conversation in the auditorium, Jud mentioned to Johnny that arrangements were being made for another session. Johnny's adrenaline was flowing— his prayers were being answered. This wasn't a one-shot thing.

During the next few months every day seemed to be another step up the ladder of success. The sight of the five strolling through the prison compound to the main gate was becoming an almost daily occurrence and, unlike before, their trustworthiness now allowed for the warden to send them out with only one guard.

"Just Walkin'" was pushing the upper reaches of record-sales charts in local and neighboring states, and there was increasing demand for the group from churches, schools, radio shows, Kiwanis Clubs, veterans and police organizations, and Nashville's best White hotels.

The warden recalls: "My booking procedure was a simple one. Either I or my deputy warden would field calls for the group's engagements. I'd then send a security officer to tell them of the performance. I never had a schedule and nothing was ever put down in writing."

One day, as they exited through the gate, the familiar white van that had become their tour bus was missing. Deputy Warden John Watt approached them and said, "You boys can't keep showin' up at these respectable places lookin' like you're gonna scare the pants off of people, so I got you a new vehicle. There it is, guard's waitin', get goin'."

The new vehicle was a big black Buick. The car probably impressed the inmates as much as it did their audiences. Watt apparently sprung for the auto out of his own pocket, and within months it would be paid for by the group's contributions to the inmate fund. Johnny recalls that Watt ". . . was the most feared man at the penitentiary, but I usually got along pretty good with him. He musta liked music."

There were other perks too. On one of their innumerable trips to the Mansion, Clement spoke to his audience of guests, reporters, and photographers about how proud he was of the Prisonaires' success and, in part repeating his message expressed the day after the group's first recording session, said, "The Prisonaires represent the hopes of tomorrow rather then the mistakes of yesterday. Songs and salvation, that's our theme."

The governor then pointed out special guest Roy Acuff, who had performed at the penitentiary many times and had asked if there was something he could do for the group. Clement continued, "I've been watching Mr. Stewart here play his heart out on that beat-up old six-string of his and I figured a hit group needs a hit guitar . . ." And, courtesy of Roy Acuff, Clement presented Stewart with a brand new $250 Gibson guitar.

With his favorite whiskey-filled coffee cup in hand, Clement, feeling elated over his quintet's rapid rise in acceptance and buoyed by each new guest convert, decided his political and policy moves could become bolder. As he would soon find out, so could public resistance.

There came a showdown. In mid-summer Edwards authorized the Prisonaires to perform at Central High School in Gainesboro for a fundraising bazaar to help pay for uniforms for the school band. He also allowed thirty-five inmates from the prison variety show, including the prison orchestra, to join in support. All but the five Prisonaires wore prison uniforms with numbers; the fearful citizens of Gainesboro must have felt they had been invaded by convicts.

The newspapers spoke out in opposition. Wardens as far away as Sing Sing in New York lambasted everything from the contingent being accompanied by only three guards to the fact that they were there at all. Newspaper editor Fred Tardy of the *Jackson County Sentinel* said it was not the type of performance to be shown to school-age children. "It not only put the students in the position of admiring and paying tribute to convicted criminals, but was also an unnecessary exposure of the students to the possibility of an attempted escape on the part of the prisoners."

Sing Sing's Warden Denno told the interviewer, "No prisoner [of Sing Sing] is allowed to go out of the prison and earn money either for the prison funds, or for himself. If you were to allow the prisoners out to earn money for the prison fund, you would be allowing a few prisoners to work for the benefit of all, and also allow the few to take special privileges not available to the other prisoners. We treat all of them alike here."

Glen Swafford, former warden of the Tennessee State Prison, commented, "We didn't let 'em go entertaining when I was warden. We wouldn't take that chance."

Though the Gainesboro engagement had been Warden Edwards' decision, the responsibility rested with Clement. Edwards recalls that during one phone conversation Clement particularly took issue with one paper's sideswipe that the governor had "declared war on Tennessee youth."

Edwards told him, "The conservatives are going to want you to shut down the reform program and the Klan is going to throw you and me on the pyre as fuel for the fire."

A local Democratic party member who visited the governor's office made the same point, saying the state was up in arms over Clement's "pet niggers."

Clement knew there was a problem brewing, but he wasn't going to give up his plans for prisoner rehabilitation. He promised, however, to keep the band under wraps and deny them access to public events. He would also have the singers keep a low profile for a while. Calling Edwards back, he nevertheless requested that the group be present at the next night's party at the Mansion: "Eddy Arnold's going to sing and of course I want the Prisonaires there. My guests are just as important as the 'Chitlin Circuit'!"

(The Chitlin Circuit was a collection of theaters and clubs that presented many of the top Black performers and only Black performers. It included the Royal Theater in Baltimore, the Howard Theater in Washington, D.C., the Apollo in New York, and the Regal in Detroit, among others.)

Though there had been no incidents at Gainesboro High School, anti-reform advocates kept up their attacks on Clement. But they lost some of their momentum about a month later, after an incident at a large Nashville performance venue.

The Prisonaires were ending another well-received show when the audience spilled onto the stage and into the backstage area. Mobbed for autographs, the singers were pulled into the crowd and became separated from their lone guard. When the quintet regrouped at the car, the guard was nowhere to be seen. Sanders believed he saw him "with a pretty young thing hanging from his neck."

The five decided then and there to take themselves for a ride . . . right back to the prison. At the gate, the sentry asked where the guard was, to which Drue, who was driving, said, "I dunno. Can we get some sleep? We got another show tomorrow." The guard waved them in and they could hear howls of laughter coming from the gate area as they drove by.

Johnny recalls: "I heard one of 'em yell to another, 'Well, the niggers are safe but the guard escaped!'"

Twenty minutes later, the missing officer called on the phone to report that the singers had fled. According to the story that later circulated among inmates, the assistant warden responded, "Fuckin' idiot, the niggers are in the pen where you're supposed to be. Next time we'll send them out to guard you. And you better learn to sing!"

U-82

Vocal
BMI

SOFTLY AND TENDERLY
PRISONAIRES
Confined To Tennessee State Prison
Nashville, Tenn.
189

MEMPHIS, TENNESSEE

Return to Hartsville

chapter ten

FOR TWO CENTURIES White South-
erners have said that, though the system in the South oppressed
Blacks, the two races understood one another, that they could com-
municate with one another. A more profound separation and mutual
alienation of the races, they said, can be found in the industrial
North—Detroit or Chicago, say, where the two groups don't com-
municate.

The situation would worsen again in the South in the '60s as
civil rights legislation began to be enforced. But popular culture,
which was national, began to soften the line that separated the races
during the 1950s.

Johnny experienced this firsthand. Inmate number 37509 never was much for cleaning up the auditorium, but he loved the assignment and the freedom to laze around when his group or the prison orchestra wasn't rehearsing. Therefore, when a guard came looking for him one day in July, Johnny was annoyed to have to accompany him to the main offices to meet a visitor from the Tennessee Bureau of Criminal Identification. Johnny also feared he was going to be brought up on some false charge and sent to solitary confinement.

The assistant warden had lent his office to a youthful, slim, White man with a Marine-style haircut who now sat behind the desk with a black attaché case in front of him. Introducing himself as James Proctor, he invited Johnny to sit down.

As Proctor leaned forward, arms extended over his case, he didn't read Johnny's fear and didn't realize the effect that what he represented would have on someone doing time. He reached into his case and pulled out a long piece of paper.

"Johnny, I wrote this song and I'd like you to listen to it," Proctor said. "I wrote it especially for your group." The situation was the opposite of what Johnny had imagined. Someone in power was coming to him for assistance.

When he recovered from the shock, he said, "Uh, okay, what's it called?"

Proctor, like a kid anxiously awaiting the car keys to pass from Dad's hand to his, wheeled around in the chair, picked up a long black sack, and pulled from it a shiny acoustic guitar. "It's called 'A Prisoner's Prayer,'" he said, as he began playing and singing the song.

Johnny soon became caught up in the equality that music creates even among *un*equals. He didn't hesitate to recommend a change here and there. The two spent an hour or so in the office, reworking the song to their mutual satisfaction. It was, in fact, a good song for the group and it was good to have it. Johnny was short a song or two for the upcoming recording session. Over the next few days, Johnny, bucket in place squarely over his head, wrote another tune, "No More Tears." This beautiful slow song, with William Stewart's trademark bouncy ballad guitar touch, deserved high marks as an example of the Ink Spots/Mills Brothers style. And it was finished just in time for their next session.

The Prisonaires continued to sing at Sunday services and on one occasion found themselves performing alongside the legendary Clara Ward Singers. Clara gave Johnny the idea to record the old spiritual "My God Is Real." That, in turn, led him to think about rehearsing another spiritual, "Softly and Tenderly."

On August 3, 1953, Sun Records' newest act and only vocal group returned to Memphis. Sixty-four days earlier they had entered the town anonymously. Now their movements were being followed closely in the press and among the public by supporters and enemies alike.

Sam was glad to see them. "Just Walkin' in the Rain" was selling well, and he was so busy filling orders that he had released only two singles since. That success couldn't have come at a better time. Phillips had issued eleven singles since Sun's inception in 1950, and only Rufus Thomas Jr.'s "Bear Cat" (an answer record to Big Mama Thornton's "Hound Dog"), with a coincidental B side, "Walkin' in the Rain," made the charts. The failures included Joe Hill Lewis's less-than-optimistic platter titled "We All Gotta Go Sometime." Lewis earned more for his session on "Baby Please" with the Prisonaires ($10) than he saw in royalties for his single.

The group had a productive second session, laying down four sides: "My God Is Real," "Softly and Tenderly," Proctor and Bragg's "A Prisoner's Prayer," and Johnny's "No More Tears."

The piano backup on "Softly and Tenderly" was anything but soft and tender. As the tune rocked along with a handclapping gospel fervor and frantic pace, the pianist seemed to have a favorite riff; he had used it before at Sun Studios, when he was the bandleader and pianist on "Rocket 88." The keyboard player was Ike Turner.

The Prisonaires' summer of '53 performance schedule was becoming increasingly busy. Many of their trips to the Governor's Mansion were impromptu and when a guard wasn't available the warden's wife, Red, or even the warden himself was their driver. Often without a highway patrol escort.

Edwards, reminded of those incidents, recalls with a smile in his voice: "John Drue [Junior] was my regular chauffeur, but I didn't realize until now that on those occasions I was his!"

That summer the Prisonaires exited the prison gate nearly every day. One performance date particularly enhanced their reputation for reliability. While waiting their turn offstage, Marcel went to the men's room. Across from his urinal was Mr. Martin, their guard, who had loosened his pants and set down his gun on top of the fixture. Finishing his business, he walked past Sanders, leaving his gun behind. Marcel left the toilet and approached Johnny. Pointing the pistol at Bragg, he asked what to do with it.

"Man, don't point that at me! Where'd you get that, anyway?" Johnny asked.

"I was takin' a piss and Mr. Martin was too. He put it up on the toilet and left without it," Marcel said.

"Put it back. See if he misses it," Junior teased.

"Aw, just give it to him. If he gets in trouble, we ain't gonna be far behind." Ed decided.

When Martin looked up from his newspaper to see Marcel standing over him with a gun, he fell off his chair. The officer got up and pulled the weapon away, looking around while shoving it back into his holster. Realizing that only the singers had seen him, he made them promise to keep their mouths shut. Johnny kept his word—for over forty-five years.

It was at an engagement in Hartsville, Tennessee—a forty-mile drive northeast of Nashville—that the group gave their most heart-wrenching performance.

William Stewart recognized every turn in the road and every house and shop leading to the auditorium where they would per-form. He was going home.

A writer from *Ebony* magazine had been in Hartsville to do a story on the Prisonaires for their November issue, and a photo that ran, of Stewart and his family with only his grandfather smiling, shows the family's heartache at not having seen William outside the prison walls for thirteen years.

When the Prisonaires took the stage that evening and launched into a few gospel numbers, they were wildly received by the packed house. But Stewart's family reunion was the real story.

The group settled into an old-time soulful spiritual, more than appropriately titled "Comin' Home." As women in the audience became tearful and then hysterical, several had to be restrained. Halfway through the set, William himself stepped back, hid his face in his hands, and bawled uncontrollably. He was totally overwhelmed by the mass outpouring. The others were barely able to finish the song. And no one, onstage or off, escaped with a dry eye. The whole performance lasted less than forty minutes, and each member left the stage emotionally drained. This time the trip back to the penitentiary was without the usual chatter of an after-performance high.

According to Johnny, "We didn't speak most of the way, but I said—to make it better—'least we got the group.' An' everyone kinda nodded 'yeah.'"

Ed Thurman had been in prison for thirteen years, Johnny Bragg for ten, John Drue for two and a half years this time around, and Marcel Sanders for two. Each of the Prisonaires had his own sense of what Stewart and his family felt.

There were other performances, too, that reminded the Prisonaires of family. The governor on occasion would lend the group out to political allies for performances. Johnny remembers playing Senator Albert Gore's house. "His son Albert Jr. was a firecracker all right. He liked to have pillow fights. One time, he had one with me, just bein' playful, and the pillows burst all over the livin' room. All those feathers were flyin'. . . ."

The Prisonaires' "Just Walkin'/Baby Please" was also flying, to number three in Nashville, number five in Memphis, and number five in Shoals, Indiana, on *Cash Box* magazine's regional R&B charts. Most important, it was at number ten on the nation's R&B Top Ten. (The number-one record at the time was B. B. King's "Please Love Me.")

Look and *Time* magazines soon picked up on the celebrity singers, and the August 12, 1953, issue of *Jet* magazine, while keeping the "gimmick" story short, wrote with an accompanying photo, "The Prisonaires, a unique quintet of singing Tennessee convicts, are the first musical unit to attract national attention while serving prison terms. . . . Their repertoire: Spirituals, Blues, Pop, Hillbilly." The group had garnered the inside front cover of *Jet,* which was, after *Ebony,* the most prestigious Black magazine in the nation.

By the end of September 1953, "Just Walkin'" remained at number three in Nashville and debuted at number six in St. Louis. The *Nashville Banner* stated that the song had sold about thirty thousand copies since it had been issued. The paper also showed the now familiar top-to-bottom photo of the five and stated that Marcel Sanders would appear before the State Pardons and Parole Board the following day, Wednesday, September 23, for a parole hearing.

It went on to say, "Sanders, who sang bass, was charged in connection with the death of Ezell Holloway during a knife fight. A navy veteran and short-order cook in civilian life, Sanders said he would like to continue in the music business when he gets out of prison, 'but don't know exactly where to start.'"

His "start" was a startling revelation to all concerned. As Sanders exited the parole hearing, Bragg and a group of convicts were coming in from the exercise field. "They let me go," Marcel said, "but I'm stayin'."

Edwards remembers vividly the phone call to the governor that afternoon. "They paroled Marcel Sanders, you know, the bass of the Prisonaires," Edwards said. "Sanders refused the parole. Said he didn't think he was ready. Said he wanted to stay with his group. They couldn't find a precedent for his refusal so they're letting him stay until they can figure out what to do about him."

Clement attributed Sanders' decision to loyalty. It was more complex, and Edwards knew it. It was also a nuisance. "The board may drop this for a while," Edwards said, "but they'll come back to it and you can bet any others up for parole aren't going to pass it up."

"But three of those men are lifers," the governor reminded him. "Besides, I never planned on this going on forever."

"Then you're going to go through with your plans?" Edwards asked.

"Course I am. Not right away, but the knockout punch for rehabilitation is getting these men out. For now though, since the time's not right, they're as good as a national TV show worth of great press for the program."

Marcel was enjoying an unexpected taste of success and privilege he'd never known before. That, plus his likely fear of returning to the real world, were as much if not more of a factor in his decision to stay as any loyalty might have been. For the time being, Sanders' apparent fear coincided with the governor's political needs and kept the singing group intact.

Edwards knew the parole board wouldn't be caught off guard again. A few days after Sanders made his stunning decision, Bob Brassell, the inmate who organized the prison variety shows, also told his parole board that he wanted to stay in prison and continue to work with the singing group. Beginning as music coordinator for the prison's variety shows, he had become, effectively, the manager of the Prisonaires.

What was astonishing about Brassell's decision was simply that he is White. The board must have found the whole phenomenon deeply unsettling. For Brassell, celebrity was apparently more important than race. Or freedom.

The parole board insisted that Brassell leave Tennessee if paroled. When he declined, they transferred him to the Fort Pillow prison farm. Realizing they were not going to accommodate him, Brassell announced on September 29 that he had changed his mind and had found a parole sponsor connected with a Tupelo radio station. He was soon gone from the scene.

September heralded the release of the Prisonaires' second single, the semi-shuffle spiritual "My God Is Real" as the A side with the lively spirited "Softly and Tenderly" on the flip side. (The number-one song at that time was "Crying in the Chapel" by the Orioles.)

By the time *Billboard* reviewed the Prisonaires' new release on October 10, "Just Walkin'" was still performing well, remaining number five in Memphis, moving up to number four in Nashville, and debuting in New Orleans at number eight on the *Cash Box* R&B Jukebox Top Ten.

Reviewed in *Billboard*'s Spiritual section, the new release garnered an impressive 74. "Softly and Tenderly" rated a 72, and the reviewer noted that the driving beat didn't overpower the song's religious feeling. Other records reviewed that day which illustrated the type of music sweeping the nation's airwaves included Nat Cole's "That's All," the Jordanaires' "Is He Satisfied?", Cab Calloway's "Hey Joe," John Lee Hooker's "Too Much Boogie," "Laughing on the Outside," by the Four Aces, and "Farewell, So Long, Goodbye," by Bill Haley (a year before "Rock Around the Clock").

Sun seems not to have had a clear idea of how to promote a spiritual. Though it was well-reviewed, overall sales on the new record were unimpressive. Sam Phillips tried a gimmick by noting on the record label, under the Prisonaires' name, "Confined to the Tennessee State Prison, Nashville."

Why Phillips, who had never issued a gospel single in his life, chose that time to follow his pop-blues hit with two spiritual sides is difficult to comprehend, especially when he had sitting in the can Johnny's Ink Spots–inspired "No More Tears" as a natural ballad follow-up to "Just Walkin'." "My God Is Real" came and went, while "Just Walkin' in the Rain" continued its popularity through October.

The first change in the group was expected to come with the parole of John Drue, on October 3. The quintet had planned for that day and agreed that Drue would continue to record and perform. With help from the warden's office, Drue could be notified of almost every Prisonaires engagement and could join them.

But Drue, for whatever reason, was denied his parole. The group, though disappointed for Drue, was relieved to be remaining intact. And had Drue gotten paroled, Warden Edwards would have missed him the most. Finding a reliable chauffeur wasn't easy.

Memphis
Music
BMI

U-85
Vocal
2:38

A PRISONER'S PRAYER
(James Proctor)
PRISONAIRES
Confined to Tennessee State Prison
Nashville, Tennessee
191

MEMPHIS, TENNESSEE

Rockin' in the Pen

FOURTEEN DAYS AFTER Drue failed to be paroled, the Prisonaires drove the now familiar route to Memphis for their third Sun session. Discographies of Sun sessions indicate that the October 17 taping included another version of "No More Tears," a song Bragg wrote called "If I Were King," and a Jennings/Brooks song, originally recorded by the Jubilaires in 1945 on Decca, titled "I Know." (The original Drifters would cover the same song in 1957.)

By the first of November, "Just Walkin'" was still number three in Nashville. On that day, Sun had reportedly printed a label with prison stripes for the Prisonaires' next 45rpm record, "A Prisoner's Prayer" (with "I Know" on the B side). "Prayer" was a mournfully sad tune, bordering on the spiritual. "I Know" was another song perfectly suited to the Prisonaires/Ink Spots parallel (here again Johnny showed a remarkable ability to copy Bill Kenny's vibrating falsetto to baritone styling on ballads) and would certainly have been a better A side.

Billboard's December 12 R&B review section thought much the same thing, as it gave the top-side nod to "I Know" with a 71 rating and a strong comparison to the Ink Spots and their ballads. "A Prisoner's Prayer" received a solid 70 rating, with kudos to the lead singer's vocal strength and a reminder to the reader of the origin of the singers. Other competing vocal-group songs reviewed that day included the Four Tunes' "Don't Get Around Much Anymore," the Five Keys' "My Saddest Hour," and the Moonglows' "Just a Lonely Christmas."

The novelty prison-stripe label didn't sell more records, and Sam Phillips's promotional efforts seem halfhearted. Though Jud Phillips was a strong believer in the act, Sam's taste for R&B was too rudimentary to fully appreciate the Prisonaires. If he had paid more attention to their sound on rockers like "That Chick's Too Young to Fry" and "Baby Please," as well as Bragg's ballad "No More Tears," he might have realized he had a solid R&B group that could have competed professionally with northern groups like the Du Droppers (RCA), the Vocaleers (Red Robin), and the Crickets (MGM), not to mention the Clovers (Atlantic)—all of whom were solid acts with varying degrees of regional and/or national success.

Instead, he was issuing singles of a raw blues nature, such as the Ripley Cotton Choppers' "Blues Waltz," Little Junior's Blue Flames' "Mystery Train," and Little Milton's "Begging My Baby." Still, the Prisonaires' tri-state celebrity status and the occasional national media curiosity kept them in the public eye.

Ebony magazine did a five-page spread on the act, with a large banner proclaiming, "The Prisonaires, unique singing group of Tennessee prisoners, wins fame on radio, TV, and records." *Ebony* seemed especially impressed by all the White venues the group was playing, and noted, "The Prisonaires have appeared on TV, sung for numerous white civic groups in Nashville's best white hotels, and are regular entertainers at the Mansion of Governor Frank Clement."

Ebony was exaggerating when it asserted, "'Just Walkin' in the Rain' has sold over 225,000 copies." If it had, the Prisonaires would have been on the national pop Top Forty not the Nashville Top Ten, and playing on Ed Sullivan's national TV variety showcase instead of on Wally Fowler's local TV show. But the inflated number probably encouraged readers to take more notice of the group.

The Prisonaires collectively were earning $30 to $50 a performance and, after the twenty-percent inmate fund contribution, the other eighty percent was to have gone into their own prison trust accounts. According to a newspaper account, however, most of their recording money went into the prison's recreation fund.

Johnny had an additional account set up at a Nashville bank for some of his songwriting royalties. Warden Edwards remembers: "I drove into town with my wife and Johnny to open a savings account for him, since the money coming in was more than we cared to take responsibility for in the prison."

As the group continued to prove itself trustworthy, the range of opportunities for performance continued to expand. Now, in addition to entertaining at the homes of the governor and senator, and at churches, schools, and service clubs, they were also performing at other parties (one for the staff of the state adjutant general, one for the National Guard), American Legion posts, county fairs, halftime at football games, night clubs, even Boy Scout jamborees, once doing backup for would-be-singer Audrey Williams, widow of the late Hank Williams.

The music of the Prisonaires bridged worlds Black and White, free and unfree. But the lives of Johnny Bragg and the others had only extremes, with nothing in the middle. They were still doing time during the days, and many evenings, but when they left the prison they were treated as celebrities.

And just as with any other singing group, for the Prisonaires there were certain special backstage benefits, the kind of benefits that seem always to be available to the guys in the spotlight: adoring fans of the fairer sex. Though they weren't called groupies back then, whenever the Prisonaires had a performance there was a familiar coterie of women who began to show up with greater regularity than chance would seem to allow.

Gentleman that he is, Johnny avoids details, but does admit, "We had some fun back in those days. We were practically free, and we always could find a little place backstage or somewhere."

One particular relationship for Johnny began after a perform-ance in a church outside of Nashville. Johnny remembers striking up a conversation with a young woman who had a younger relative in tow; the youngster, about fourteen, was named Annie Mae. The woman and Bragg hit it off and she began showing up at a number of his shows. On some occasions she brought Annie Mae. Years later he learned that the young Annie Mae Bullock grew up to be his former session musician Ike Turner's wife, Tina Turner.

At year's end the group once again made the newspapers. But this time it wasn't their singing that gained them attention. En route to a church performance on Christmas Eve, their car, with Thurman at the wheel, cut in front of and sideswiped another auto, driven by James H. Baird, a city fireman.

The damage to both cars was insignificant, but their traveling guard, Mr. Martin, decided to take Baird into a nearby house and report the accident. Johnny remembers the tense moments when the group sat alone in the parked car on a dark Nashville street.

"Well, whadda we do now?" asked Marcel.

"We don't do nothin'. You plannin' on doin' somethin', William?" Bragg huffed.

"Not me," Stewart responded.

Junior was thinking it over. "I think . . . we could all just walk away. I mean, if we wanted to."

Johnny answered loudly, "Ya' know, you walk, you bury all of us. . . . Your time'll come. Hell, you only got a few years. We got forever."

With five minutes gone since their custodian disappeared, Thurman eased the tension by breaking into song.

When Mr. Martin and Baird stepped back onto the street, they could hear the strains of "Crying in the Chapel" coming from inside the car.

Saturday, December 26, the *Banner*'s headline read, "Prison Singers Left Unguarded, Aide leaves quartet alone to phone after wreck." The news report did manage to partially qualify its sensational headline by paragraph five, where it noted, "Warden Edwards said, referring to the damage to Baird's car, 'I'll get it fixed and it will only cost about $1.00.'"

On February 2, 1954, the Prisonaires returned to the Sun Records studio. Sam, still searching for something he could relate to, recorded three sides: a new, catchy, up-tempo, Robert Riley composition, "Don't Say Tomorrow"; a third try in three sessions on "No More Tears"; and "I Wish," a beautiful ballad mixing elements of the Orioles, the Ink Spots, and the Ravens.

When the *Nashville Tennessean* ran a new story ten days after the Prisonaires' Sun session, it turned up the tension a few notches between the singing group and their less-privileged fellow convicts. The headline "Visit Ban Excludes Prisonaires Quartet [*sic*]" covered the report that an order from Keith Hampton, the state commissioner of corrections, requiring direct permission for outside visits by state prison inmates would not apply to the Prisonaires. Inadvertently, Warden Edwards' belief in prisoner rehabilitation had almost jeopardized the Prisonaires' performance opportunities.

Hampton, a political appointee and former political leader in Marion County, said in the article, "The Quartet [*sic*] consisting of four [*sic*] long-term Negro prisoners will be allowed to continue booking engagements for personal appearances outside the prison." Hampton compromised by allowing Warden Edwards to continue activities with the Prisonaires in exchange for a crackdown on what seemed to Hampton, and some of the public, to be Edwards' growing tolerance for other outside activities.

Hampton had issued the orders concerning outside visits several days earlier, following disclosures of at least two "visits" beyond the walls, during which inmates admittedly sought aid in arranging their own releases from prison. Those disclosures were followed in short order by reports that two other long-term murderers had lived for five months in an unguarded pump-house bungalow, outside the walls of the prison. On Hampton's orders, these two convicts were put back behind the walls.

Some inmates were beginning to feel that all the attention given the Prisonaires was focusing attention on those trying to circumvent the system. An undercurrent of resentment toward the singers kept growing inside the penitentiary. But, at the same time, other inmates saw the Prisonaires as a light at the end of the tunnel, and by 1954 there were more than fifteen different vocal ensembles in the penitentiary.

On May 8, 1954, Sam and Jud Phillips packed some heavy, cumbersome recording equipment into a vehicle and drove the 190 miles to the Tennessee State Penitentiary.

A few nights earlier, Edwards had had the singers come to his house to entertain for a few guests. Before the performance he announced that there was about to be a very historic event—the Prisonaires were going to do a recording session in the prison.

Johnny Bragg was ready. "I wrote two songs just for this 'n and I believe we had a hit here," he says, remembering that day.

Sam set up his two-track recording equipment in the auditorium. The group filed onto the stage in their prison stripes, which must have been a momentary shock to Sam; he'd never seen them in anything but suits. Two guards, feet up over the seats several rows back, were the group's only audience. They did two versions of "What'll You Do Next?" featuring Marcel on bass lead in a call-and-response style.

Full of harmony, the up-tempo romp with only guitar and a long-since-forgotten convict on bongos, sounded a little like a Drifters' tune, still a year in the making, titled "What Cha Gonna Do?" The second song, "There Is Love in You," was a handsome ballad and the only Prisonaires recording written by Bragg with co-writer William Stewart, who was also the featured vocalist. Sam felt he might have something he could sell from that session and assured the group they would have another single shortly.

What happened later that same month would forever impact Johnny Bragg's financial future.

Joe Johnson, a music publisher working for film cowboy and country singer Gene Autry's Golden West Melodies, contacted music publisher Red Wortham at Autry's request. Gene had been one of countless stars who had performed at the prison in 1953. The Singing Cowboy remembered hearing Johnny and the group do "Just Walkin' in the Rain" at an inmate show, and when their recording hit the charts he made note of it.

Wortham had acquired the publishing rights to "Just Walkin'" as his part in the deal that originally brought the Prisonaires to Sun Records. Autry always liked the song and, feeling it could have a life after the Prisonaires, bought the rights from Wortham. Not long after the Golden West song acquisition, Autry reportedly recorded a version of "Just Walkin' in the Rain" for Columbia Records. (If so, it has long since been lost or filed away).

Red Wortham apparently had squeezed out what he thought was all the money in the Prisonaires' record and therefore felt he had little to lose. Johnny believes that much of the money the group made went into Wortham's pockets.

Bragg now says: "Sam [Phillips] was a good man. He'd use 'nigger' all the time, but tha's just the way he'd talk. Sam was an honest man. He paid Red Wortham, and Red Wortham beat us out of the money. The royalties we was s'posed to get was s'posed to go into our account. I could tell you this, that most of the money that was s'posed to come to [me] from royalties or otherwise, went in someone else's pocket."

It was nearly fifteen years, according to Johnny, before Wortham admitted he was not only receiving publishing and writing royalties, but he was also getting the group's artist royalties from Sun.

On July 1, 1954, the Prisonaires' fourth and last Sun single was released. As Sam Phillips had promised, the songs were from the prison recording session, with "There Is Love in You" as the A side and "What'll You Do Next?" on the B side.

Billboard reviewed it on July 17 as a spiritual release, surprisingly, since the songs were basically pop and R&B. "There Is Love in You" earned a 73 rating and was considered a "pretty ballad." The review noted Stewart's baritone lead and considered it one of the Prisonaires' best, speculating it could gain airplay and would be popular on jukeboxes. "What'll You Do Next?" earned a 69, but the reviewer felt their vocals lacked emotion, even though the beat was strong. The review also mentioned where the group was imprisoned.

Other musical milestones reviewed that day included Bill Haley and the Comets' "Shake, Rattle and Roll" (Joe Turner's version was already number one on the R&B charts), Petula Clark's "The Little Shoemaker" (ten years before America knew her for "Downtown"), the Clovers' "I've Got My Eye on You," Marvin & Johnny's "Cherry Pie," Ray Charles' "Don't You Know," the Ravens' "I've Got You Under My Skin," the Orioles' "In the Chapel in the Moonlight," and the Flares' "This Is the Night for Love." All outsold the Prisonaires' single.

As with the previous singles, "There Is Love in You" began getting play locally on Nashville and Memphis radio, but sales were sporadic at best. Sam Phillips's attention was also diverted by the new artist he'd been searching for, a White kid who could sing like a

Black man, who was now cutting his first master for Sun, only four days after the release of the Prisonaires' new record.

This new artist was Elvis Presley—the dust-covered teen who'd been looking for a break at Sun Records but ended up helping Johnny with his diction on "Just Walkin'"—and the song was "That's All Right."

In fact Presley's record began competing with Johnny's when Sam issued "That's All Right" on July 15, just fourteen days after the quintet's single hit the streets. The timing for the emergence of an artist like Elvis coincided with the success that a few White disc jockeys (like Alan Freed in Cleveland and Dewey Phillips [no relation to Sam]) were having playing Black artists' R&B records to both White and Black listeners.

Dewey, who was a fast-talking, high-energy jock on WHBQ (the nighttime call letters for WDIA) in Memphis, had caught Sam's imagination. He saw Dewey's success with his *Red, Hot & Blue* show as a sign that if he could find a White man who could sing in an R&B style, he'd have radio acceptance because he had something unique. He had no idea how big a crossover concept he had.

In mid-summer, the ever hopeful Prisonaires were back in Memphis recording four more songs for Phillips.

Though they had a distinctive sound of their own, elements of their favorites—like the Ravens, Clyde McPhatter and the Drifters, and the Ink Spots—could also be heard in their records. Despite the group having crafted some fine recordings, Johnny began to realize that the Prisonaires needed to alter their instrumental sound in order to compete more favorably with what was selling.

Up to that point, almost all their recordings had only acoustic guitar accompaniment, with an occasional piano, bass, or electric guitar. Johnny decided to use some of the prison band members for the session and so, for the first time, there was a real backup group for the singers—Hubbard Brown on drums, George Williams on trumpet, Henry "Dishrag" Jones on piano, and an unknown electric guitarist.

Among the compositions were "Lucille, I Want You," a terrific Drifters-style, mid-tempo, boogie-woogie rocker, written by Bragg and Sanders, and "Two Strangers," another Robert Riley ballad, with Johnny doing his best take yet on the falsetto of Ink Spots' lead singer Bill Kenny. They also taped a beautiful, blues-styled number, "Friends Call Me a Fool," written by Riley and Bragg, featuring Johnny who switched to a brilliant Clyde McPhatter, high-tenor, ballad sound, while the Prisonaires did a commendable Drifters harmony.

They also recorded a song written by Bragg as a tribute and musical telegram to Governor Clement, titled "What About Frank Clement, a Mighty, Mighty Man." It was sung in the chug-a-lug, "shouting in the tabernacle" gospel style, and seemed to scream "If we flatter you, will you let us go?" (It wasn't the first specialty song Bragg wrote for him, but the others had been at the request of the governor.)

Johnny often discussed topical songs with Clement in their meetings in his library when the governor would commission, so to speak, Johnny to create an event song such as "Tennessee Scene," a song describing the state, or "Boast for Texas" which the Tennessee leader wanted to use to poke fun at Lyndon Johnson's former Senate campaign manager (and future Texas governor), John Connally.

Clement was riding high in the Democratic primary race that August but was by no means a shoo-in against his old adversary Gordon Browning. Browning, like Clement, had politics in his blood and didn't know how to stop running. He had been campaigning for a generation; the babies he kissed in his first campaign were now old enough to vote for him.

In April of the prior year, the state legislature had lent an unintentional helping hand to the Prisonaires and the new governor when they had met to commence a limited revision of the oldest unamended constitution in America. One upshot was the decision to increase the governor's term from two to four years, effective with the 1954 election.

Clement was actually playing for bigger stakes. Former President Harry Truman was wavering on a decision to run again in 1956 and, while the Missourian pondered, Tennessee's Senator Estes Kefauver threw his hat in the ring to Truman's everlasting chagrin. Truman's animosity toward "Senator Cowfever," as he called him, made for a natural alliance with Governor Clement. Publicly, Truman stated that Kefauver was "a nice man and a good senator." Privately, he referred to him as "that fella from Tennessee that was aching to be president and went around getting his picture taken in a coonskin cap."

But Clement also had other possibilities in mind. He had given money to various churches over the years, helped raise funds for Billy Graham's crusades, and often served as a lay preacher. There had been occasional speculation by politicans, friends, and family that Clement was tempted to relinquish the power of the state's highest office and become an evangelist.

Bob Clement remembers: "Billy Graham had approached my father to give up politics and join his crusade but my father said, 'The best way for you to help the people is your way and the best way for me to help them is mine.'"

Whatever deep calling Frank Clement felt, he put it aside for the time being and went head-to-head with Browning.

At the end of the century "Southern liberalism" seems like a contradiction in terms. A public figure like Clement is assumed to have some motive for advancing progressive causes in spite of a conservative constituency. But Clement was an advocate of racial justice and penal reform because of his faith in the possibility of spiritual renewal as well as his sense of right and wrong.

That summer Clement needed a thick skin as former governor Browning began an extremely negative campaign. Browning referred to Clement, just as he had in earlier campaigns, as "a liar," "a pipsqueak," "a demagogue," and a "loud-mouth character assassin." The wider the gap between them developed, in terms of personality, the more sarcasm Browning added to his vitriolic speeches: "The young ex-FBI agent could not track a bleeding elephant in six feet of snow. . . . He had been in two wars without ever locating a battle. . . . The young man," Browning would bellow, "would not be able to locate the right end of a horse for a halter."

Clement, stumping in his trademark, broad-brimmed white hat and white suit, often with a contingent of country musicians, took the high ground. In spite of the personal attacks, he remained congenial. His skin seems to have been watertight to criticism, as he rejected any thought of personal animosity. He preferred to attack his opponent's record. Clement would indict Browning for his political favoritism and his neglect of the blind, handicapped, and aging.

He defended his own candidacy by noting Browning's mudslinging and "the vile names he has bitterly spewed in my direction merely because I have had the temerity to seek the office he considers his own." He would invariably end a speech with pulpit fervor, "Precious Lord, take my hand, lead me on." The line from the hymn became his slogan, his verbal signature.

The attacks on Clement took their toll. His son Bob says, "My dad treated these things like water off a duck's back, but my mother took the criticism very seriously." The sheer nastiness of politics, and of the verbal and written abuse, eventually drove Lucille further into depression.

On August 5, 1954, Clement won a landslide victory in the Democratic primary, carrying all but one of the state's ninety-five counties. Because the Republican party in Tennessee was practically nonexistent, the primary race was the one that counted. The November general election would be a cakewalk.

But it was not going to be an easy election year for any Southern progressive. In May the U. S. declared school segregation unconstitutional. Southern politicians had two choices: they could come out against desegregation, defying the inevitable confrontation with the federal government, or they could indicate that the law could not be ignored but that compliance would be cautious, calculating, and as limited as possible. The radical first course created the risk that constituents would assemble in violent, racist mobs. Frank Clement stood for cautious compliance.

He declared that all Tennesseans were bound to recognize the Supreme Court's decision, though he left the problem of implementation up to lower-grade local school boards. By January over a thousand members of the White Citizens Council and the Ku Klux Klan, many in white sheets and cone-shaped white hats, marched on the state capitol to demand the governor oppose the Court's decision or abolish the public school system. Hoping to avoid mob violence, Clement invited three of the crowd's leaders to a private meeting.

Three hooded men were escorted up the steps by the officers as the mob outside shouted racist slurs. Clement was a Methodist lay preacher as well as a smart politician. The Klansmen found him in his office with a priest, two Protestant ministers, and a rabbi. He invited the representatives to join them in prayer. The Klansmen said they hadn't come for spiritual guidance. But Clement told them he would pray about all their concerns.

He was in his best evangelical form, delivering one of his favorite Bible quotes, Micah 6:8. "He hath showed thee, O man, what is good; and what doth the Lord require of thee, but to do justly, and to love mercy, and to walk humbly with thy God?" Then Clement asked for a prayer from the rabbi.

The Klansmen were stymied. They stormed out, unable to engage the governor in the conflict they wanted. Clement soon moved to the capitol entranceway. He spoke to the mass of protesters, saying, "A governor who submits to pressure rather than follow reason would not be worthy of the office. . . . Strife breeds more strife, violence produces more violence, and agitation causes trouble where none would otherwise exist. I cannot please you today because I don't think the course of action you suggest is in the interest of Tennessee." Placards drooping, the mob moved on.

In May 1955 the Supreme Court issued an order requiring that the states implement desegregation with all deliberate speed. Governor Wallace of Alabama would stand in a schoolhouse door in defiance. Frank Clement's deliberate pace and relatively nonconfrontational approach would keep federal troops out of his state when rioting was erupting in others.

And so, while trying to advance a flickering career and working through their personal dilemmas, this quintet of R&B singers in Tennessee, defended by a political figure under intense pressure, moved toward the center of an immense social and political movement that would ultimately engulf the entire country for decades.

The story of the Prisonaires would be more conventionally dramatic if they were the most successful group in the country. But—and this is a part of the inside story of all artists—they were having real struggles with the details of refining and shaping their talents so that their audiences would continue to want to hear them, and those promoting them would continue to see reasons to do so. By the summer of 1954 the quintet was a long way from the top. It wasn't at all clear that the Prisonaires could succeed. In fact there were signs that Sun's support had waned.

Sam Phillips scheduled "Two Strangers" and "Friends Call Me a Fool" for release in September, even assigning matrix numbers (U-132 and U-133; used to keep account of each recording slated for pressing) to the anticipated release.

But by then Elvis was number one on the Memphis charts and raising hell with his leg-and-body movements in local performances. Presley had signed a recording contract with Sun Records on July 12, and on September 9 came back to Sun to record several takes on a single, "Good Rockin' Tonight." With all the excitement over Presley, Sam seems to have been too preoccupied to pay much more attention to the Prisonaires. Their "Two Strangers" single was never pressed.

"Seems every time we hit a home run, God would throw a pitch at my gut just to remind me who's runnin' the show," Johnny recalls. On September 5, 1954, he received news that his father was dying and Warden Edwards allowed Johnny, with a security officer, to go to Nashville's Veteran's Hospital.

Wade told his son that he'd been following his career with the Prisonaires and that he was proud of him. "I turn on the radio and it's like a visit from ya. Truth is, since you started, I never turn the radio off. Don't you stop what you're doin'. It means somethin', it'll get you through this. . . . Don't you stop."

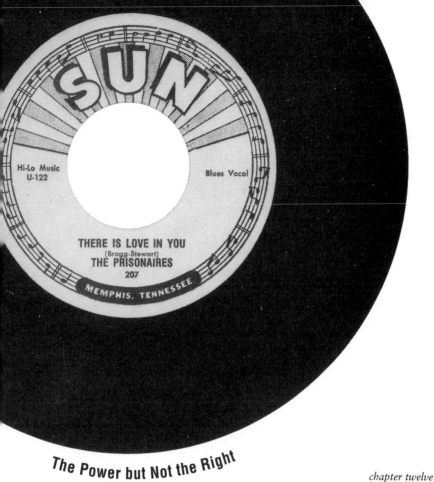

Hi-Lo Music
U-122

Blues Vocal

THERE IS LOVE IN YOU
(Bragg-Stewart)
THE PRISONAIRES
207

MEMPHIS, TENNESSEE

The Power but Not the Right

JOHNNY PERSEVERED. HE continued to look for ways to bring his group into the R&B and pop mainstream. At the seventh Sun session in early fall Johnny had honed the Prisonaires into a ballsier R&B group.

On this session they again had the support of a few members of the prison orchestra, picked up like session musicians. They recorded "Surleen," a gospel/rocker written by Bragg, with secular lyrics and a jive-talking middle; "All Alone and Lonely," a contagious rhythm/rocker also written by Bragg, with a scat-era sound (and piano by Ike Turner); and the sex-saturated mover with a six-bar bridge of early rock, "Rockin' Horse," also by Bragg.

Just as happened earlier, when Johnny and the group were recorded over the Pat Boone radio show, the reuse of recording tape resulted in the kind of anomaly that collectors and trivia buffs live for: Sam Phillips, who was thrifty, decided to record the three Prisonaires tunes over outtakes from another artist's session rather than use clean tape on an act for which he had few hopes. Though the Prisonaires never had an opportunity to record *with* Elvis, they unknowingly recorded *over* him, as bits of "We're gonna rock, rock, rock" from "Good Rockin' Tonight" could be heard on the reused tape between the quintet's songs.

While the Prisonaires continued to seek a niche in music culture, they would have to adjust to changes within the group. The fall session at Sun was the last done by the original members. They had made twenty-two recordings of nineteen songs. It would take music historians decades to unearth the Prisonaires' contributions and to begin to see them as pioneers of southern vocal-group R&B and doo-wop.

Until the Prisonaires appeared, most singing groups of the recording nobility were out of the northeast coast (Dominoes, Clovers, Orioles, Ravens, Crickets), the Midwest (Flamingos, Moonglows, Spaniels, Dells, Midnighters), or the West Coast (Robins, Platters). Although the Five Royales, the Larks, and the Drifters (all from the Carolinas) first made records before the Prisonaires, all made their names recording secular music after being discovered in New York City. Acts like the Tempo Toppers, from Texas and featuring a youthful Little Richard on lead, recorded after the Prisonaires' success.

Furthermore, acts like Bobby Mitchell and the Toppers from New Orleans, recording in the spring of 1953, and the Clefs from Arlington, Virginia, recording in 1954, failed to have a success equal to that of the Prisonaires'. The only other southern vocal group to do well during that period was the Spiders from New Orleans, but their first chart hit (number-three R&B) was not until February 1954 ("I Don't Want to Do It").

The dissolution of the group began suddenly. The Prisonaires were rehearsing in the auditorium on October 6, 1954. Marcel was inexplicably absent. Midway into the rehearsal he appeared, exasperated. He told the group that this time the parole board had kicked him out.

It had been over a year since Marcel first refused parole; this time the board wouldn't let him stay. It was a rare situation and not even his friends knew how to react. No one had ever heard of an inmate being kicked out. The board told Marcel that he had been an embarrassment to their system and they wanted him discharged right away. Johnny walked over to Marcel, put an arm on each of his friend's shoulders and said, "We'll miss you, but it's time to go home. No more room and board. You evicted." The Prisonaires had lost their bass.

Two months later another member was released. Late one night Junior Drue, who was in his cell next to Johnny's, began to whisper after lights out.

"Ya know, we ain't hardly heard 'Softly and Tenderly' on the radio lately or 'A Prisoner's Prayer.'"

"They're still playin' 'Just Walkin'' . . . what you gettin' at, Junior?"

"'Just Walkin'' is gonna die off too . . . I'm leavin'. They're parolin' me. What you gonna do now?"

"Replace ya, I guess," Johnny said. If not sentimental, he was certainly tenacious.

Drue seemed deeply offended. Johnny is sure that Drue believed he was irreplaceable.

The pieces were falling out of place. But Johnny had a strategy to maintain continuity and to keep his own work alive. As leader of a group now recognized nationally, Johnny had his pick of other talents. There were by now, he estimates, as many as twenty singing groups organized inside.

"I'd go 'round the prison and listen to the other groups, and I'd pick someone who could do it all [tenor to bass] . . . who could sing better 'n me, and when the time come, I'd pick my replacements."

By January of 1955 the Prisonaires' remnants were Johnny Bragg, Ed Thurman, and William Stewart—the three who had started it all, years before. Willy Wilson now sang bass instead of Marcel Sanders. John Drue was replaced by Hal Hebb. Johnny formed a particularly strong friendship with Hebb. "He could dance and play them spoons. He was a helluva whale of an entertainer. He was crazy but he could sing all right."

(Hebb has another footnote in pop history: In 1963, released from jail, he was killed in a mugging. His younger brother wrote the song "Sunny" as a memorial and it became the number-two pop and number-three R&B hit as sung by Hal's younger brother, Bobby Hebb.)

That January, Frank G. Clement began his second term as governor, and Johnny got the opportunity to originate a musical work as if he were Clement's very own modern-day minstrel. He rose to the occasion with a spirited song summing up voter feeling: "We Thank You Frank for Coming Back." The title seems right for this political Billy Graham; for Clement, the voice of the people was the voice of God.

Winning the election was part of some larger scheme. On being inaugurated, and as if a reminder of his view of the power of God in politics, the governor, grandiose and fundamentalist, sent autographed Bibles to every member of the state legislature.

Clement began his term with a full plate of difficult issues. The impossible task of dealing with political pressure for desegregation would have been enough. But Clement, a proud progressive, had helped polarize politics in Tennessee. He had to fight political battles over reapportionment and to outmaneuver an increase in labor unrest, bootlegging, and gambling. Clement's conservative enemies played for keeps.

His son Bob notes: "My dad had many threats made against his life. There were no gates around the Mansion at the time and state troopers were everywhere. At times we'd have fifty troopers, one behind every tree." Clement himself had no apparent fear of these threats and often went where the trouble was, despite his advisers' warnings. Bob remembers, "There was a lot of labor agitation at the time and a sheriff in Polk County had been killed. Dad went there to help quell the unrest. He spoke to the people, having been informed that just about everyone in the audience had a gun. . . . The police had no trouble after he talked to them."

It wasn't always easy for Frank Clement to reconcile his responsibilities with his conscience. Nothing, apparently, burdened Clement as heavily as presiding over death row executions. Edwards says that Clement agonized over every one of them. His emotions, sensitivity, and family upbringing put him in direct conflict with the state law on capital punishment.

His grandfather, State Senator James Archibald, opposed the death penalty and had helped repeal the capital punishment law in 1915, but it was reenacted by 1917, after a highly publicized crime. Between

1915 and 1960, eighty-five Black men and thirty-nine Whites were put to death for crimes ranging from rape to murder.

Clement, like a number of present-day politicians, seems to have been particularly fearful that he might allow the execution of an innocent man. He took an evangelist's approach to making himself sure of their guilt.

According to Warden Edwards: "The governor officiated at five executions while I was warden. In each case the condemned men espoused their innocence repeatedly prior to their judgment day and in each case, after the governor spoke with them, they admitted their guilt."

Before one particular execution date, Clement visited the inmate's cell and heard a confession from him. Nothing in the case justified a stay of execution. That Black man, Harry Kirkendall, along with a White man, had murdered a sixty-three-year-old gas station attendant in a robbery—for $600. After spending an hour and a half with Kirkendall, Clement with his wife, Lucille, exited the prison. On their way they passed a Black woman with her little children.

In Clement's own words, as quoted in Lee Seifert Greene's book *Lead Me On*: "I'd never met them, but there couldn't be any question. . . . As I went on by them I rationalized my thoughts, I thought . . . well, they may not want to see me at a time like this. . . . I got to the front gate and I stopped and I told my wife that I can't do it. She said, 'What?' I said, 'You know who those children were?' She said, 'I think I do; I'm afraid to say.' I said, 'Why that was Mrs. Kirkendall and her six kids. I can't do it, I've got to go back and talk to her.'"

The governor ushered Lucille and Mrs. Kirkendall and her family into the warden's office. Clement's own description of the encounter shows a vulnerability unusual in a political figure: "[I said], 'Now, Mrs. Kirkendall, I've got the power to save your husband, but I haven't got the right to do it.' And she didn't argue with me. She sat there and tears would come down her cheek, with no outcry, no nothing. Finally, I just broke down completely, just completely, and my wife came over and comforted me till I got stabilized again. And the chaplain prayed with us.

"Then I said, 'Mrs. Kirkendall, do you want me to talk to your kids?' I took the youngest one on my lap and I talked to them. 'There are some things that the state cannot forgive you for, but God can forgive you for anything.' . . . I talked to them and . . . kept my composure. I promised their daddy . . . that I'd see that they got the best Christmas they ever had and that everything my boys got we shared with them. Then I sent her a little bed, bed clothing, and everything else, and we've been in touch with them since then and helped them."

He described the execution of another murderer, Charley Sullivan, who had been convicted with Kirkendall, as a sort of opportunity for spiritual salvation. Clement continued: "[Sullivan said] 'I know everybody thinks I'm going to crack up and I'm scared to death . . . tell them not to put any handcuffs on me and let my arms swing free.' We walked down and I said, 'Sure we'll do that.' He walked and sat in the chair. After they started putting on the straps he said, 'Let me stand up again please.' They let him up again, he knelt down, put his head in the chair, and prayed, got back up and said, 'I'm ready to go.'"

Though Clement loved the glare of the spotlight and the microphone in his face, on that occasion there were no reporters or cameramen in attendance; some of the flamboyant politician's most dramatic moments were never intended to be witnessed by the public.

To Frank Clement, execution—like incarceration—must have seemed intolerable even if it was seen as a means to transformation, a means by which a criminal was reconciled with God.

It is likely that whatever political gain Clement hoped to achieve by promoting the Prisonaires, the greater gain was a belief that he could help them become better citizens and better men.

But his expectations, at least for some of them, may have been too high. On February 5, 1955, Johnny, William, Ed, and new members Hal and Willy were exiting in their street clothes through the gate for what was by now a routine performance. Three guards were escorting a group of new prisoners into the yard. As the groups passed each other, Johnny noticed a familiar face and called out, "Junior, what are you doin' here?"

Junior Drue smiled and answered, "Looks like one to two." He'd only been out about three months.

"What'd ya do?" Ed asked.

"A little house breakin'. Ain't you glad to see me?" Drue asked.

Johnny thought, "Well, the warden'll be happy. He's got his driver back."

Now the group sometimes rehearsed and went out with as many as six or seven members. As the membership changed, so did the group's name, though Johnny no longer recalls all of the aliases. It wasn't until their next recording opportunity that they took on a new name permanently.

By the beginning of March of 1955 the lineup was drawn from eight major players: Bragg (lead and tenor), Thurman (tenor), Stewart (baritone), Drue (tenor), Hebb (tenor), Wilson (bass), and Henry "Dishrag" Jones, who had played piano on the last two Prisonaires recording sessions for Sun Records. L. B. McCollough, a nonsinging guitarist from the prison orchestra, joined later in 1955. Each new member had to pass muster with Warden Edwards.

The act continued to be popular on radio. They were also doing television shows and public events, in addition to performances at the Governor's Mansion. These men were scarcely doing hard time, and Clement and Edwards continued to gamble considerable political influence by giving Bragg and his group so much freedom.

While the membership was shifting, Robert Riley came up with an easygoing rocker he called "Rollin' Stone," and Johnny loved it. Hal Hebb, however, felt the song deserved to be sung by a group with a more upbeat, positive name. So they began to call themselves The Sunbeams. (Brand names in the music business during the '50s were not prized. Groups sometimes changed names when personnel changed slightly, when careers stalled, when they went to a new label, or even, as in this case, to suit a particular member or record label executive.)

Around this time Red Wortham, knowing that the Prisonaires' deal at Sun was ended, brought Ernest L. Young to the prison. After hearing the group do "Rollin' Stone" and a few other tunes in the auditorium, Young was impressed enough to tell Wortham they had a deal and to bring the group to his studio.

Excello Studios was part of Young's Nashboro Record Company and its affiliate, Excello Records of Nashville. The label started in 1952 as a gospel company, but was heavily into R&B by the time the Sunbeams were formed.

On March 3, 1955, Johnny's full cast drove into town with their usual single, armed escort. They arrived at Excello's 177 Third Avenue address and went immediately to work. The mambo and other Latin rhythms were becoming tremendously popular at the time and Young found "Rollin' Stone" a perfect fit for the Latin beat, while taking the tempo up from the group's audition rendition. The Sunbeams also laid down a pop R&B shuffle titled "Why Don't You" and a Latin shuffle, originally recorded by the Prisonaires a year before, titled "Don't Say Tomorrow." Johnny's vocal was mixed out in front of the harmonies. Unlike the original, done with only guitar accompaniment, the Sunbeams' track included drums, bass, piano, maracas, and guitar in a slower tempo.

Although more commercial, harmonically it was not as pleasing as the original. The differences were of little consequence; neither surfaced as a single. (Only the Prisonaires' recording of "Don't Say Tomorrow" ever reached the vinyl stage, when a compilation LP of their Sun sides was issued in the 1990s on Bear Family Records [Germany, 1990] and later on Charly Records [U.K.].)

The Sunbeams recorded four takes of "Rollin' Stone" that day and take three was the issued A side, with "Why Don't You" on the flip side. With two new members, the Sunbeams had a looser harmony than the Prisonaires, but Johnny's voice remained unique and it was maturing.

Sometime between the session and the record's release in April, Johnny renamed the group again, this time calling them The Marigolds; he felt Sunbeams was too prissy for a group of prisoners. The new group was just beginning to gel when once again it changed. One sunny day in April, while jogging around the prison's track, Johnny was approached by Stewart.

"They're pardonin' me, Johnny. Ya believe it? The governor's givin' me a pardon. No more ninety-nine!" Stewart was going home to Hartsville.

Again showing his tenacity and lack of sentimentality, Johnny picked Stewart's replacement within minutes. He approached a quintet near the wall, practicing an R&B piece called "Fate Has a Brother." Listening intently, Johnny waited for a pause and said, "Al, got a minute?"

Al was Alfred Brooks. He was a lifer—a better prospect, long-term—in prison for killing a schoolteacher when he was seventeen.

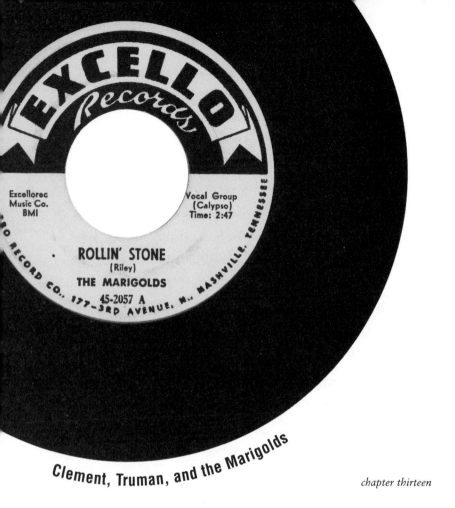

Excellorec
Music Co.
BMI

Vocal Group
(Calypso)
Time: 2:47

ROLLIN' STONE
(Riley)
THE MARIGOLDS
45-2057 A
177—3RD AVENUE, N., NASHVILLE, TENNESSEE

Clement, Truman, and the Marigolds

IN HIS WAY, Johnny Bragg had achieved a novelty celebrity status that often made him feel anything was possible. One such instance was the night of April 24, 1955.

On the way to an apparently routine event at the Governor's Mansion, Warden Edwards behind the wheel, they all noticed a larger security contingent than usual, including a group of well-dressed, secret-service types mixed in with state and local police. Convincing anyone that six Negroes in a black Buick had any business at the residence that night was not easy. Only when a regular Mansion guard noticed that the car was driven by the warden was the group led in under escort.

Edwards, not wanting to give the singers time to get nervous, waited until the last possible minute to tell them they would be singing for former President Truman, who was the governor's special invited guest.

The Marigolds, most of them newcomers to the Mansion, got the jitters immediately, and as they sat over dinner in the kitchen the tension mounted. Most were still getting used to church and club congregations. Even Johnny, who'd been singing for two years in front of most every kind of audience, realized this was going to be a once-in-a-lifetime experience.

When the singers were summoned, they walked into the empty drawing room on the first floor and grouped in front of the baby grand piano. A portrait of Andrew Jackson looked down from over the fireplace as the guests filed in, including the governor's arch rival Senator Estes Kefauver, former President Harry S. Truman, and Truman's daughter Margaret, along with other dignitaries.

Governor Clement towered over Truman as they talked while the other guests took their seats in a semicircle around the Marigolds. Johnny remembers overhearing Clement proudly telling Truman about his steps to bring about prison reform.

Then the governor introduced the group (which he continued to refer to as the Prisonaires). They began with the spiritual "Carrying the Cross for My Boss"; one couldn't help but wonder if they were singing about God or the governor. For the next half hour they sang a variety of songs, including "This Old House," "Amazing Grace," and "Lead Me On," Clement's favorite hymn.

Clement had requested a song from Johnny, dedicated to the former president, and the group had rehearsed one for weeks. Now they sang the tribute. After the initial surprise, the president and guests laughed and applauded the unabashed accolade. It was a huge hit.

After a short break the Prisonaires returned to find Margaret Truman at the piano, and she accompanied them as they sang "The Old Rugged Cross." Too shrewd to let such a golden moment pass, Clement suggested the group perform the "Missouri Waltz," the president's favorite song. With the president's daughter still at the piano, the group sweetly harmonized the 1914 standard. Bob Clement and Johnny both remember seeing tears in the president's eyes.

"What do you think of my boys, Mr. President?" Clement asked.

"I think you oughta pardon every damn one of 'em!" Truman said emphatically.

The thought had already crossed the governor's mind.

Frank Clement was an early riser. He was up especially early the following morning, the first work day of the week, since he'd had such a special guest sleeping over. At 5:30 A.M. he was filled with excitement as he knocked at the door to the president's room. He knew that the former chief executive also rose early and was surprised when he got no response. He opened the door and discovered that the president was gone.

Bob Clement, the governor's son, remembers: "My dad tore down the hall, grabbing one security man after another, but no one had seen him. Dad was frantic." There were numerous nightmarish possibilities; Clement even asked one trooper if the Prisonaires had stayed over.

"He ran out the front door, down the drive, into the street," Bob says. "He ran down Curtiswood Lane [the winding country road in front of the residence] and saw this short, briskly moving figure heading away from the Mansion. Sure enough, it was Mr. Truman. My father about fired five security people, right there on the spot!"

When Clement, secret service men and troopers far to his rear, caught up to Truman his imagination took over. As Bob's father later told him the story, the conversation went something like this:

"Mr. President," Frank said, puffing, "where you going, sir? Is anything wrong? Tell me who agitated you and I'll have his head for breakfast."

"Governor, you're interrupting my constitutional!" Truman indignantly responded.

"Mr. President, this here's Nashville. You can't take a constitutional alone in Nashville!"

"Well, you see me doing it, don't you?" the president shot back. Then, for the first time, Truman looked over at the governor. "Frank," he said, "where the hell are your clothes? It's not proper for a potential vice-presidential candidate to be running around town in his robe."

Truman had read Clement's mind and the governor was grateful. Clement could not succeed himself as governor. The only way for him to move up in politics was to win a seat in the U.S. Senate or to lobby for a shot at the vice presidency.

Truman and Clement had hit it off extremely well. During a speech by the former president to a throng of cheering Tennesseans, Truman said, "I am proud to have your governor call me his friend; I am his." The governor knew he could do worse than hitch his star to Truman, especially as the 1956 Democratic hopefuls were buzzing around the former chief executive, hoping for his endorsement, and Clement now felt he was in the running.

Two days later the local newspapers reported "Clement Frees Prisonaires' Tenor, Commutes 99 Year Prison Sentence for Davidson Countian." Ed Thurman was the fourth Prisonaire to be released, and the second to have his sentence commuted from ninety-nine years to instant parole.

Johnny had heard about it accidentally on April 25, a day before the announcement, when the warden met with him in the visitors' room to discuss—the day after their *last* visit—the group's *next* visit to the Governor's Mansion. It would be their two hundred ninety-fourth. (According to Bragg, Ed kept track of such things.)

Edwards had his own methods for communicating with the group, and with Johnny in particular: "I never would meet with any of the group individually in my office. I didn't want to show any partiality, so if I needed to convey a message to Johnny, I'd send a security officer or meet him in the visitors room."

As Bragg was leaving, Edwards said to him, "By the way, I was just informed that Ed Thurman's sentence has been commuted by the governor. He'll be free in two days. I would guess you'll need to look for a new singer." Johnny was by now used to recasting.

A few hours later Johnny saw Thurman heading for the auditorium. He said to him, reflectively, "We sure done it all, ain't we?" Thurman replied, "My two strengths here have been God, and you naggin' at me to practice."

Johnny, looking straight-faced at his longtime partner, simply said, "Practice is over." And then, Johnny says, they hugged. "I never remember huggin' any man, but I hugged him."

Politically, Clement's timing in releasing Thurman was poor. It gave fuel to his foes, who saw his meeting with the president, the group's performance at the Mansion that Sunday, and Tuesday's announced release of Thurman as more than coincidence. When questions arose about the Prisonaires being at the Mansion on Sunday night and whether or not the governor had promised Thurman he would intervene for him, Clement didn't answer.

Warden Edwards, according to newspaper accounts, publicly denied knowledge that his group was at the Mansion at all that night, and said that he had been at the Ramp Festival in Cosby, Tennessee (which he had been at earlier in the day with Truman and the governor). The state commissioner of corrections, Keith Hampton, also disclaimed responsibility. For once, no one wanted to take credit (or responsibility) for the singing group's activities or whereabouts.

The parole board had actually taken up the question of Thurman's release in February, two months earlier, when prison officials and the prison chaplain had asked for clemency. The board was about evenly split between advocates of reform and hard-liners. It seems likely that Clement chose to publicize Thurman's release when he did in order to benefit from the recent presence and support of the former president, who was known to be an advocate of rehabilitation regardless of the heat from the press.

On April 29 an article appeared in a Nashville newspaper, with the caption "Songbird out of a Cage." It went on to lambaste the governor, the parole board, and other liberals for what the writer considered abuse of their authority in letting a man go who would normally not be eligible for parole for some fifty years.

When Clement responded, he stated, "Thurman had become a Christian in his fifteen years in prison, and he would become a valuable citizen when released." That response—in which Clement claimed the religious high ground—infuriated his opponents.

The columnist argued that the governor and the parole board had overridden a trial. He said, in effect, that it was frightening to think that a talent for singing should allow a convicted murderer to go free after serving only fifteen years of a ninety-nine-year term. But the writer ignored the prejudice of the all-White jury and also ignored the fact that Thurman's crime was a hot-blooded retaliation, not a cold-blooded murder. (Thurman killed the man who had slain his dog.)

The article's closing remark was another stinger. Encapsulated, it stated that based on what they had seen, Tennessee's inhabitants could only hope that the killers still in prison can't sing.

The early April release of the Marigolds' first record was reviewed in the April 30 issue of *Billboard,* only one day after the angry newspaper column. "Rollin' Stone" was given a 72 and was classified as a novelty song with a good beat. "Why Don't You" received a 69 and was considered an acceptable interpretation of a nice ballad. Bill Kenny of the Ink Spots had a new release, "If We All Said a Prayer," reviewed the same day.

Other memorable works reviewed on April 30 included Fats Domino's "Ain't That a Shame," the Flamingos' "When?", Hank Ballard and the Midnighters' "Switchee, Witchie, Twitchie," Howlin' Wolf's "I Have a Little Girl," and the Feathers' "Why Don't You Write Me?" All were heavy competition for an R&B hit chart that held only twenty spots at the time.

"Rollin' Stone" was soon getting airplay and its chart numbers rose. By June 4 it was number six in Atlanta and number one in Charlotte, North Carolina. More important, it burst upon the national scene that same week, reaching number fifteen on the *Billboard* R&B bestseller list. In coming weeks it would climb in Los Angeles (number five on July 2), the Baltimore–Washington area (number six, July 16), and New Orleans (number six, July 16). On

June 11 it had rolled to number twelve as an R&B national bestseller and stayed on the charts nine weeks. Most chart books of later decades state that it reached number eight, but the weekly *Billboard* national lists of the time indicate its high-water mark was number ten (July 23) on the national jukebox listings.

On July 16 Elvis Presley had his first chart hit as "Baby Let's Play House," on Sam Phillips's Sun label, reached number-five jukebox and number-ten bestseller on the national country charts. Johnny took considerable notice, and even had a feeling of pride upon hearing the news.

The author of "Rollin' Stone," Robert Riley, was in for a welcome surprise. The pop trio the Fontane Sisters, of New Milford, New Jersey, latched on to his raunchy song and rode it to a pop-chart debut on June 4, and eventually to number thirteen nationally. Though the Fontane Sisters' cover record was a pop hit far outselling the Marigolds' version, it lasted only six weeks on the charts, three weeks fewer than the original. The Cadets also covered the Marigolds' moneymaker.

The early summer of 1955 saw the Marigolds back at Excello, hoping to repeat their debut success. Johnny had written his most pop R&B-oriented number since "Just Walkin' in the Rain," an upbeat rocker titled "Love You–Love You–Love You" (similar in style to the Jewels' "Hearts of Stone").

"Love You" was coupled on the session with Robert Riley's "Two Strangers," which the Prisonaires had previously recorded for Sun Records but which was never released. They also recorded two other sides that day that were forgotten about for many years. The new single enjoyed a July release and was an R&B "spotlight pick" in

Billboard's August 13 issue. Calling the group "versatile," the review described "Two Strangers" as an original and absorbing ballad, and praised the performances on "Love You."

Another single was released that day by Excello, this one by a group called the Solotones. The ultra rare, up-tempo, blues-tinged single came to light in 1999 through the efforts of music historian George Moonagian who noticed that on his copy the writers of "Front Page Blues," the B side, were credited as Robert Riley and another inmate, Leon Luallen, and that on the flip side, "Pork and Beans," the writing was credited to Johnny Bragg. Moonagian also noted the tremendous similarity in the Solotones' and Marigolds' sounds, as well as the uncanny resemblance of the Solotones' lead singer to Bragg.

When I asked Johnny about the song, he brightened immediately and, before he was played the record, sang one side and then the other of the forty-four-year-old single. After hearing the 45, he confirmed that these were the two mystery cuts done by the Marigolds. Apparently Ernest Young at Excello had decided to issue the record under a fictitious group's name, hoping to win interest for an act that didn't exist. If it took off he would quickly put together a new group, as was the practice at the time.

Some memorable competition for the Marigolds' "Two Strangers" was also released that day, notably the Turbans' "When You Dance," the Nutmegs' "Ship of Love," Shirley & Lee's "Feel So Good," and Joe Turner's "Midnight Cannonball."

Prison life, which was most of the daytime hours for Johnny and the other singers, remained grim as ever. Home was a six-by-eight cell. They ate in the dining hall and worked in the shops.

In extreme contrast was the heavy schedule of rehearsals, performances on radio and before live audiences, and recording sessions. The Marigolds can't help but have daydreamed about a full-time life outside, about full-time freedom.

Johnny recalls, "We used to play at it, we had so much freedom. We said, 'Man, looky, we're free. We could just go if we wanted to.' We said back to ourselves, 'Yeah, but we ain't gonna do that though. Nah, we ain't gonna do that.' We never abused the privilege, not one time. We were trustworthy, but we thought about it lots of times."

Another distraction the Marigolds came up with was what the group called "making phone calls."

"We'd be out somewhere performin', go backstage, or waitin' to come on, and one, then another, then another, they'd go to make a phone call. The guard, he'd let 'em," Johnny recalls. "I'd go to see what was goin' on, and they'd be callin' up the open end of a whiskey bottle!"

From fans to friends, to those just being neighborly, getting the entertainers a drink became routine. If they could drink under the nose of a symbol of the law, so much the better.

By the standards of other inmates, the Prisonaires had enviable lives. But Johnny was increasingly unhappy. His good fortune was compromised by watching other members of the group be paroled.

The contradictions in his life weighed on him—he was the last original Prisonaire, in his twelfth year of confinement. His frustration surfaced on one of his visits to the Governor's Mansion. After the group finished their show, he asked the governor for a private audience. Clement told Johnny to meet him in the library.

Johnny waited. The room was filled with photos of Clement with celebrities, politicians, even one with Johnny Bragg. There had been many other talks in this room between these two, on subjects from religion to music. They had become familiar with one another.

When Clement arrived he offered Johnny a seat, lit his cigar, and, after he noticed Bragg's hesitancy, said, "Come on, you know the rules—in here, just you and me. You're free to say whatever you want." Johnny remembers what he said, though he'd not known how to express his own feelings until he heard Clement's words.

"'Free.' That's my confusion, Governor. I'm free to sing for a president, go places, do things I never imagined. I'm free to live better than any man has a right to in prison, but I ain't really lived what it's like to be free. Now Thurman's free, Stewart's free, Sanders is free. Drue, he been free so many times he can't keep track. Couple of those guys killed people. Johnny Bragg didn't kill no one. Johnny Bragg didn't rape no one neither! Is Johnny Bragg ever gonna be free?"

Clement started to answer. Johnny, clearly beside himself, interrupted the governor. "You don't know *what* I feel. I got family I can't be with. I got a father, died waitin' for me. I never cared cuz I thought since the time I came here at seventeen, this is the way it's s'posed to be. Ninety-nine means ninety-nine. I got six ninety-nines but guys with ninety-nine, you're lettin' 'em go . . . and I'm not one of 'em." Johnny pounded his fist on Clement's desk.

Clement took it all in. But he told Johnny that he wasn't playing games with the prisoners' lives, wasn't just spinning a bottle and freeing whichever man it pointed to. The governor explained that he sincerely hoped to get every well-meaning man out of the prison and into a decent job and life so he wouldn't come back. He reminded him, with emphasis, of the obvious: that every time he let a convict out early, like Stewart or Thurman, he risked having his enemies try to shut the door for good. Clement didn't think that the state was ready for a convicted rapist, innocent or not, to be pardoned. And he didn't know if it ever would be ready.

By now Clement was also agitated. Standing up, he leaned forward in direct eye contact with Johnny and unintentionally broke his cigar in two.

According to Clement's son Bob, when Lucille came into Frank's office the next day he told her about how Johnny Bragg had finally blown his lid. He said he knew that Johnny had a point, but the governor couldn't even give him hope. Not in the Tennessee of 1955.

However much discontent Johnny felt, it's not surprising that he was envied. A number of prison guards and inmates were growing ever more resentful about what they considered Bragg's entitlement program.

A sophisticated (by prisoner standards) scheme was devised, with the intention to discredit Johnny. One day a convict nicknamed "Yeller" began to spread the word that Johnny was his partner in dealing cocaine to inmates. The word came to Johnny in the commissary, through Henry "Dishrag" Jones.

When the lunchroom bell rang Johnny got up, tucked his metal cup into his waistband, and walked to the door. He found Yeller in the yard. Without a word he jumped the con, and using the cup as brass knuckles, repeatedly struck him in the face. Several guards pulled the two men apart. The yard boss ordered the guards to clear the yard and to take Bragg to solitary.

Johnny recalls: "I had to go to the dry cell for three days cuz he said Johnny Bragg was backin' his cocaine sales." Johnny actually spent only one night in solitary confinement, but not because the warden was lenient. He was let out of solitary because the quintet was needed for a performance that night. And that just provoked more bad feelings toward Johnny.

A few weeks later Johnny was caught in a much more serious fight—one that could have ended his singing forever.

During a rehearsal, a message came to the auditorium that the chaplain wanted to see him. Johnny walked to the northwest end of the prison courtyard and entered the chapel. In a side hallway he was jumped by four White inmates. He knocked one down but the other three wrestled him to the floor. Then one of them pulled out a two-pronged, foot-long garden tool.

"Say goodbye to your singing chords, *nigger*. When I'm done, you won't be able to even sing for your supper."

The blade was at Johnny's throat when Drue, Brooks, Dishrag, and Wilson rushed through the door. By himself, Drue slammed two inmates into a wall, and the other singers jumped in to beat off the others. The scuffle ended quickly with the attackers running for the back door.

"After you left," Brooks explained to Johnny, "the reverend came round. Said he never asked to see you. Came to ask what we were gonna sing at tomorrow's service."

After that close escape, the Marigolds stuck together for protection. By the fall it was apparent that their "Two Strangers" record released in July was going nowhere, but the group was in heavy demand to perform. One of the countless bookings on their agenda was a place Johnny knew very well.

It was in another life that Johnny had hung out at the Cotton Club (formerly the Nashville Cotton Club), collecting empty bottles for show fare. The evening the Marigolds arrived for their performance, memories of even the smells—of empty whiskey bottles and the sweat of performers running back and forth from their dressing rooms— came back to him.

Fifteen years earlier Cab Calloway had bounced Johnny from his dressing room. Now, as they entered, an oversized bouncer showed the Marigolds a room where they could wait until they went onstage. It would be a while. The group's guard sat in the corner reading the paper, while Hebb and the others chattered away about the women in the audience.

"Okay if I make a phone call?" Johnny asked Mr. Martin. It was an unusual request; Johnny wasn't a drinker and never made "phone calls." "Sure, go ahead," said Martin without moving his eyes from the horserace results.

Johnny walked down the hall to another room. It didn't look much different, he thought, but then he really only remembered the black, circular garbage can and the big, dark wood door. He sat down for a minute by the mirror surrounded with light bulbs, and recalled Billie Holiday bursting in on him, and the empty whiskey bottles he was collecting, and what she said to him. He sat silently for minutes, a wide smile forming across his face, and finally said, "Thank you very much, Miss Billie. Thank you."

The Marigolds performed every rock'n'roll and R&B tune they could think of that night, and even threw in a few hillbilly and pop songs for good measure. Johnny pushed his vocal limits as though Billie Holiday were auditioning him once again. It was a spiritual turning point.

When they left the club, Johnny didn't mind where he was going; he focused on the fact that he'd returned in triumph to his starting point. He says that from that day forward he never went beyond the

TOP: 1962. Lucille Clement, former President Harry Truman, and Governor Frank Clement during Clement's third run for the governorship. COURTESY OF FRANK G. CLEMENT FOUNDATION

INSET: 1952. The Clement boys surround candidate Clement and Mrs. Clement in this promotional flyer used during the lawyer's initial bid for elected office. L–R: Bob, Gary, Frank, Lucille, and Frank Jr. COURTESY OF FRANK G. CLEMENT FOUNDATION

BOTTOM: 1963. A Thanksgiving photo of the Clement family taken in front of the Governor's Mansion, with some of their barnyard flock. L–R: Frank Jr., Gary, Bob, Lucille, and Frank. COURTESY OF U.S. CONGRESSMAN BOB CLEMENT ARCHIVES

TOP: 1963. Bob Clement, Governor Frank Clement, and President John F. Kennedy at a rally only months before the president's assassination. COURTESY OF FRANK G. CLEMENT FOUNDATION

BOTTOM LEFT: AUGUST 13, 1956. Governor Clement on the front cover of *Newsweek* magazine. COURTESY OF © 1956 NEWSWEEK, INC. ALL RIGHTS RESERVED. REPRINTED BY PERMISSION

BOTTOM RIGHT: 1956. Warden Edwards and his family posing in front of the Tennessee State Prison. TOP TO BOTTOM: Warden James "Droopy" Edwards, Evelyn "Red" Edwards, Joyce, and Jim. COURTESY OF JAMES E. EDWARDS COLLECTION

FACING PAGE: 1955. Warden Edwards on the phone (probably fielding another call for the services of the Prisonaires). COURTESY OF JAMES E. EDWARDS COLLECTION

TOP LEFT: 1963. The Jordanaires, along with the acts shown here that performed at the Tennessee State Prison with the Prisonaires. COURTESY OF BROADCAST MUSIC, INC. ARCHIVES

TOP RIGHT: Hank Williams. COURTESY OF BROADCAST MUSIC, INC. ARCHIVES

CENTER: Little Jimmy Dickens. COURTESY OF BROADCAST MUSIC, INC. ARCHIVES

BOTTOM LEFT: Gene Autry. COURTESY OF GENE AUTRY ENTERTAINMENT

BOTTOM RIGHT: Roy Acuff. COURTESY OF BROADCAST MUSIC, INC. ARCHIVES

TOP: Elvis Presley in a rarely seen candid photo at a recording session, with unidentified musician, circa mid- to late-1950s. Elvis intersected Johnny Bragg's life on more than one occasion. COURTESY OF BROADCAST MUSIC, INC. ARCHIVES

RIGHT: 1955. Sam Phillips at work at Sun Studios. COURTESY OF SHOWTIME ARCHIVES (TORONTO)

FACING PAGE: 1950S. One of many publicity photos of Governor Frank Clement. COURTESY OF
FRANK G. CLEMENT FOUNDATION

TOP: 1953. A triumphant Governor Frank Clement stands with family and friends at his inauguration. L–R: Carl Nicks (Frank's uncle), future senator Ross Bass, Ida Clement Nicks (Frank's aunt),
Mr. and Mrs. Robert Clement (Frank's parents), Bob Clement (Frank's son), Governor Clement and
wife Lucille, Anna Belle Clement (Frank's sister), and Gene Clement Peery (Frank and Anna Belle's
sister). COURTESY OF U.S. CONGRESSMAN BOB CLEMENT ARCHIVES

BOTTOM: DECEMBER 12, 1956. Johnny Bragg receives his BMI award for "Just Walkin' in the
Rain." L–R: Robert Riley, Bragg, Warden Bomar, and Joe Johnson and Troy Martin of Golden West
Melodies Publishing. COURTESY OF BILL GOODMAN AND KEN FIETH, METRO ARCHIVES, NASHVILLE

TOP: The sprawling and fearsome edifice known as the Tennessee State Penitentiary, with its Gothic-tower entrance. COURTESY OF BILL GOODMAN AND KEN FIETH, METRO ARCHIVES, NASHVILLE

BOTTOM LEFT: 1972. Johnny Bragg holding the light of his life, his less-than-a-year-old daughter, Misti, while standing alongside the love of his life, his wife, Gail. COURTESY OF BILL MILLAR COLLECTION

BOTTOM RIGHT: JUNE 8, 2000. Johnny Bragg performing in Memphis at the premier of the A&E TV special on Sam Phillips. (Among those onstage with Johnny were Ike Turner, Sam Phillips, and Jerry Lee Lewis.) COURTESY OF TROY GLASGOW thought that his life, as it was, was better than it had ever been. Even if he lived in a prison, he felt lucky.

He began to rethink his resentment over not being pardoned. On his next face-to-face encounter with Governor Clement, the two began rebuilding their friendship.

Toward the end of 1955, Clement made one of his numerous unscheduled visits to the prison. He had instituted a policy of providing Bibles to all the inmates, inscribed "As a reminder that the wisdom of all the ages may be found therein." The governor spoke with many prisoners and prayed with many more.

Johnny recalls that when it was his turn to speak to Clement, the governor asked, "How are you feeling, Johnny?"

Johnny knew that the governor was referring to their last meeting. "I'm a lot better now. You were right 'bout not knowin' when or even if I'd get out. Only God can pick the right time for me."

Clement, pleased to see Johnny's return to the fold, so to speak, asked him to pray. And so they did.

To lighten the mood, the governor told him that the warden's staff had taken to calling Edwards' office the PBA, the Penitentiary Booking Agency. "He spends more time fielding show offers for you than running my prison," Clement said. "However, since I don't pay him extra, I'll let him keep doing it . . . and you keep doing what you're doing."

In late February 1956, James Edwards' tenure was coming to an end. Though she'd played her role brilliantly and bravely, the warden's wife wanted to raise their family in a more conventional setting. Edwards knew that with the governor's support he could find decent work elsewhere.

Johnny more than anyone would be sorry to see him go, and he was worried about what kind of man would take Edwards' place. Would the "slavin'" days of prisoner beatings return? Would the performances stop?

Named to replace Edwards was Lynn Bomar, a former Vanderbilt University football star. To Johnny's relief, Bomar was a rehabilitation zealot from the Clement camp, who had no intention of removing the celebrity spotlight that Edwards had focused on the Prisonaires.

In March the Marigolds returned to Nashville, tracking two more sides for Excello, "Foolish Me!" and "Beyond the Clouds," about the same time that Elvis Presley's "Heartbreak Hotel" was enjoying its eight-week run at the top of the charts.

Back on January 28, Elvis had made his first nationally televised TV appearance from New York on *Stage Show*, hosted by Tommy and Jimmy Dorsey. Elvis had performed his new recording, "Heartbreak Hotel," and Carl Perkins' "Blue Suede Shoes," and when interviewed stated, "I don't know anything about music. In my line you don't have to."

The Marigolds didn't have a chance to watch it; they had been off performing at a VFW hall. When Johnny heard about it, he couldn't have been happier. He reasoned, "Doesn't surprise me. If Presley could help *me* back then, he *must be* talented."

The Prince of Wails

chapter fourteen

THE DEAD-SONG file at Columbia
Records is similar to those at other companies: it's only as dead as
the memory of the man who controls it.

That man in Nashville, Don Law, had a keen sense of recall and
a good ear for songs. Though Gene Autry's 1954 recording of "Just
Walkin' in the Rain" seems to have been forgotten, Law remembered
the beautifully simple version by the Prisonaires. He took the song,
along with a few others, on a New York trip.

Upon seeing his counterpart Mitch Miller at Columbia's New
York City office, Law passed "Just Walkin'" over to him. The timing
was impeccable, as Miller was scouting songs for Johnnie Ray.

There were similarities in the lives and careers of Johnny Bragg and Johnnie Ray. Both men were heavily involved with vocal groups (four of Ray's six top-ten hits up to 1956 were with the Four Lads, and thirteen of his twenty-two charters were with either the Lads or the Buddy Cole Quartet). And both had suffered sensory losses in childhood. Bragg had been blind; Ray was partially deaf all his life. He had worn a hearing aid since his early teens.

Ray was a classic '50s crooner who packed so much emotion into a song that his nicknames ranged from "Crybaby" to "The Prince of Wails." Born in 1927, he was first discovered in 1951 by LaVern Baker and her manager, Al Greene, and later by Detroit disc jockey Robin Seymour. Ray signed with Columbia's Okeh label and had his first hit in late 1951, a two-sided, two-million seller ("Cry" was number one and "The Little White Cloud That Cried" was number two) with heavy vocal support from the Four Lads.

What set him apart from the typical White singer of the day was his soulful R&B influence ("Cry" also reached number one R&B). Ray had hit the pop charts twenty-three times through 1955, but hadn't had a top-ten hit since 1953, when "Somebody Stole My Gal" was number eight.

On June 29, 1956, Ray had worked his way through a tedious late-night recording session. The last song attempted was "Just Walkin'" and he finished it in two takes.

As the summer of 1956 was coming to an end, Columbia issued Johnnie Ray's version of "Just Walkin' in the Rain," backed by the Ray Conniff Orchestra and Chorus. His melodramatic version reached the charts on September 1 at number ninety-four. By October 27 it was number two on the Top 100, number two on the nation's juke-boxes, number three on the bestseller lists, and number three on the disc jockey charts. The week "Just Walkin'" was number two, the number-one song was Elvis's "Don't Be Cruel."

Ray's tearjerker wasn't confined to U.S. success either; it topped the charts in England and peaked at number six in Germany, both in December of 1956. The Bragg/Riley composition spent an incredible twenty-eight weeks on the Top 100 and nineteen weeks on the charts in England. Cover recordings of the tune by Jerry Wallace (Mercury) and Dick Richards (Columbia) added to its hit legitimacy. And in an era when sheet-music sales were still a viable income source, Ray's version of "Just Walkin'" reached number three.

As of the 1990s, it was still Columbia Records' third-biggest-selling single of all time and the number-nine bestseller among male solo artists of the rock era. It also held its own against the best of the golden age of rock'n'roll, reaching number six for 1956 and number-fourteen bestseller of the 1950s, having sold several million singles worldwide. An article in the September 8, 1956, issue of *Billboard* noted that because of the success of Ray's version, Sun Records had reissued its original recording by the Prisonaires, but its release did little compared to Ray's.

Only when he heard it on the radio did the man in cell five, Walk Ten have any inkling that his tune was a national hit. "I had a premonition somethin' big was gonna happen with that song," he says years later, "but I didn't know if it was cuz of prayin' all the time, or cuz the song was so good." Then in unselfish reflection he ponders, "I wonder if any of the Prisonaires know 'bout this?"

As Johnny was growing more successful, Frank Clement was preoccupied with political matters.

Back in February, President Truman had praised Clement as a "grand young man who would make a good vice president." Almost immediately, Clement backers had started lobbying for him to be the keynote speaker. When Buford Ellington, Clement's commissioner of agriculture, and Herbert Walters, the state's Democratic Party chairman, announced the Tennessee delegation's full support for Clement as a favorite-son candidate for the vice-presidential nomination, it significantly upset the plans of Senator Estes Kefauver of Tennessee, and forced Senator Albert Gore Sr. into a cautious wait-and-see mode.

Clement, apparently not ready for a head-to-head confrontation with Kefauver (and preferring an unrestricted delegation), stated he would not seek the favorite-son candidacy and, in an apparent trade-off, Kefauver lieutenant Charles Neese soon endorsed Clement for the keynote post. Clement couldn't have known at the time, but his choice to pursue the keynote speaker's role was the best he could do. He was unlikely to have gotten the full support of Truman, who saw Clement mainly as a foil against Kefauver.

In order to become the keynote speaker, Clement had to win over the arrangements committeemen who would pick the speaker. To show his oratorical skills, Clement made a point of addressing their state conventions wherever possible. Key party members were opposed to Clement's vault into the limelight and his chances were waning, until Truman returned from Europe and threw his weight in the governor's favor.

When the choice for that prestigious assignment came to a vote in July 1956, the governor's politicking paid off. He fielded a bloc of seven committeemen, beating out Robert S. Kerr of Oklahoma and Senator Hubert H. Humphrey of Minnesota. Despite considerable political insider wrangling earlier that year, Clement was given the opportunity to deliver the keynote address at the Democratic National

Convention in Chicago on August 13. But that also meant he was out of the running for vice president.

(The behavior of the Tennessee delegation at the 1956 convention is a history of often-misguided changes in direction. Delegates withdrew support from Kefauver, thinking he couldn't win—it looked as if John F. Kennedy would win—and had thrown their support to another favorite son, Albert Gore.)

After the Tennessee delegation had withdrawn their support from Kefauver, the National Convention nominated him to run alongside Democratic presidential hopeful Adlai Stevenson. In the end, Clement's keynote-address victory was mitigated by the success of his archrival, Kefauver.

Frank Clement approached the convention as if he were undertaking a military campaign. He flew to Missouri to consult with Truman for advice on the big campaign issues. He talked with Senators Sam Rayburn and Lyndon Johnson, as well as Democratic Chairman Paul Butler and House Majority Leader John W. McCormack, about Republican weaknesses in foreign policy. He listened carefully to Senator Richard Russell on what was going wrong at the defense department.

These were the expected maneuvers. The unexpected was his attention to the minutiae. Clement reviewed newsreels of former keynote addresses, carefully noting what touched off audience reaction and applause. He sent aides to Chicago weeks ahead to check his entrance route and his path to the podium. He analyzed blueprints of the three-foot-by-four-foot platform where he would address the convention, including the placement of microphones and TV cameras.

The governor even conferred with lighting technicians to see if his favorite white debating suits were appropriate (they were not and he unhappily wore a blue shirt and blue suit), and he arranged to have a room nearby made available for him in which to meditate prior to his speech. After all, Clement felt, his performance that night could determine if he remained by the blue rivers and red clay hills of Tennessee or went on to greater national prominence.

When the convention met on TV, some fifteen million households were tuned to Chicago. Following a film narrated by John F. Kennedy extolling the accomplishments of the Democrats, Clement strode through the smoky bustle and confusion to the podium to deliver the most important speech of his career.

Frank G. (as he liked to be called), veteran of a thousand campaign addresses, gripped the lectern and delivered an emotional, full-fledged assault on Republicans in general and President Eisenhower and Richard Nixon in particular (calling Nixon the "Vice-Hatchet Man"), and from time to time iterating the refrain "How Long, O America?" After forty-five minutes denouncing the sins of the Republican party, Clement finished his almost evangelical speech with his signature line, "Precious Lord, take my hand, lead me on!"

Clement's speech was delivered with the same fire-and-brimstone passion he had used time and again to sway his Tennessee constituents. But as sister Anna Belle states, "It was not his best speech. They [the Democratic speechwriters] made him rehearse his speech many times and narrowed it to coincide with all elements of the party platform. I've listened to hundreds of Frank's speeches and he never rehearsed any of them. He was at his best when he was totally spontaneous. His appearance on the Jimmy Dean show at the time was a better speech."

Clement's preaching style may have sung in Southern ears like gospel songs, but the new national TV audience, privy to the face and voice as one, likely found the speech, the arm-waving, and vigorous head-and-shoulder movements off-putting and even pretentious. Though his speech was not a catastrophe, it was also not a leg up for Clement's hoped-for future in the national spotlight. (*Newsweek* described him as a "political Billy Graham.")

After his speech, there was no stampede by the convention to nominate him for the vice presidency, as had happened in 1948 after delegated had heard Alben Barkley's keynote address. Clement's ambitions were, at least for the time being, stalled. When the literal and figurative smoke of the convention cleared, the ticket of Stevenson and Kefauver was approved. In the end, though the democratic process was served, the convention's choices were not the public's choices as Eisenhower steamrolled to reelection in the presidential election in November.

The Marigolds' release in March of "Foolish Me!", backed with "Beyond the Clouds," hadn't even rated a review in *Cash Box* or *Billboard*. Its one distinguishing feature was the credit on the label which read, for the first time, "Johnny Bragg and the Marigolds."

In September 1956 Ernie Young released Johnny Bragg and the Marigolds' fourth single, a full-fledged rocker and arguably their best side: "Juke Box Rock and Roll." From its pounding opening in the style of Frankie Lymon and the Teenagers' intro to "I Want You to Be My Girl" to its "Rock Around the Clock" bass riffs and scintillating sax solo, "Juke Box" was a definite contender.

Both *Billboard* and *Cash Box* reviewed it on September 29. *Billboard* plugged "Juke Box" as the top side (only crediting Bragg), while *Cash Box* was just as complimentary toward its A-side preference of "It's You Darling, It's You." The *Cash Box* review said:

Johnny Bragg and the Marigolds pair a couple of exception-ally strong sides, "It's You Darling, It's You" and "Juke Box Rock and Roll." The "It's You Darling" etching is a soft, slow-paced ballad lovely, that Bragg projects beautifully. A tender love song, given a moving performance. The flip, "Juke Box Rock and Roll," is a complete change of pace. Bragg and the Marigolds rock a quick beat jumper with the sound and feeling that has the kids crazy today. Exciter with the beat demanded. Very good deck, but will take a chance on "It's You Darling." (Translated from its music industry, '50s trade-paper lingo, the record was an up-tempo rocker with an exciting, insistent beat.)

That September day also saw the release of tough competition in records by Big Maybelle ("Mean to Me"), Lloyd Price ("Forgive Me Clawdy"), the Cadets ("Dancin' Dan"), and Paul Anka's debut disc, "I Confess," backed by those same Cadets.

To say the record crashed and burned on takeoff would imply Excello made an effort to launch it, which isn't the case. They were probably overextended with releases by Lightning Slim, Lazy Lester, and Lonesome Sundown—artists more attuned to Excello's sales strengths, as solo artists seemed to be the label's forte.

By the time the run of "Juke Box" was considered over, Bragg's occasional co-writer Robert Riley's stay at Old Red was also over. On October 18, 1956, Riley's sentence was commuted and on October 22 he was paroled. (He would go on to sign with Nashville's Tree Music as a staff writer, with recordings by artists ranging from rock'n'rollers like Hank Ballard and the Midnighters and soul artists such as Ted Taylor to country/pop acts including Roger Miller.)

"Juke Box" would be the Marigolds' last chance at recording, and it was Johnny's last hope for a hit as an artist while in prison. By the time he realized the single was a failure, he seems to have been distracted by the glory of having a number-two national hit as a writer, thanks to Johnnie Ray.

By late 1956 Johnny had been in the penitentiary for over thirteen years and was accustomed to receiving mail from fans and even other artists. The invitation he received in November, however, was a significant marker of his continuing success. The card read:

The Officers and Directors

of

Broadcast Music, Inc.

request the pleasure of the company of

Mr. Johnny Bragg and Guest

at dinner

on Monday, the third of December

Nineteen hundred and fifty-six

at seven o'clock in the evening

Grand Ballroom

Hotel Pierre

New York

R.S.V.P.

589 Fifth Avenue   Black Tie

BMI had determined that his "Just Walkin' in the Rain" was one of the year's most programmed songs on radio. It was the highest formal recognition for his accomplishments that he had ever received.

"I was just knocked out," Johnny says. "I knew it was a hit, but to be one of the biggest, I couldn't believe it. My heart felt good. I thought about my daddy, he'da been proud. And Thurman and Stewart and the others, I hoped they heard about it. I wondered if Riley went. I would've liked to, o'course, but it just didn't happen."

It's difficult to imagine what the person who addressed the invitation might have been thinking. It was likely sent to the penitentiary without anyone realizing that Bragg was a prisoner. The incongruousness of the success Johnny had begun to enjoy was probably as difficult for others to understand as it was for him.

Though he missed the BMI honors and awards dinner in New York City, Johnny did receive the BMI citation of achievement from the song's publishers, Golden West Melodies—in the warden's office.

Both Johnny and a visiting Robert Riley were met by Golden West Vice Presidents Joe Johnson and Troy Martin, along with Warden Bomar, reporters, and *Nashville Banner* newspaper photographer Bill Goodman, to capture the BMI presentation on film. The award was a great triumph for Johnny. No one could remember any convicts in American history who had been so successful while confined, and Bomar wished to memorialize the moment.

The new year of 1957 had barely started when the Marigolds were booked into a recording session at the RCA Victor Studios in Nashville to sing backup for rockabilly and country singer Charlie Feathers. This was Feathers' second recording session for King Records.

On one song, "Nobody's Woman," the group only clapped their hands, but Johnny and the rest of the group can be heard on three other songs recorded that day—"Too Much Alike," "When You Decide," and "When You Come Around."

Not long after the Feathers session, Johnny saw another of his crew get ready to go out the penitentiary gate as a free man. John "Junior" Drue was paroled on February 2 for the final time. Johnny remembers waiting in the yard as Junior walked out of the parole hearing room.

Drue said, "They're lettin' me go."

Johnny asked, "You gonna be back?"

"Likely as not," Drue answered. "The warden got me a job chauffeurin', so maybe this time I won't need to go stealin'."

Not long after, Johnny was once again summoned to the warden's office. He recalls Warden Bomar saying, "We've received a royalty check for you from the Johnnie Ray people. We're gonna put it in your trust account. You wanna see it?"

Excitedly, Johnny looked and, after seeing the amount, nonchalantly said, "Well, why don't you just put it in my candy fund. I can get some sweets when I want to."

The warden exclaimed, "You want me to put this in the candy fund! Did you see how much is here? It's $1,400, boy!"

Johnny took another look and almost fell over. He had thought it read $14. The second royalty check from Ray, later that year, amounted to more than $7,500.

Excellorec
Music Co.
BMI

Popular
Vocal Group
Time 2:34

TWO STRANGERS
(Robert S. Riley)
THE MARIGOLDS
45-2061

Presley Comes and Johnny Goes

JOHNNY BRAGG HAD come a long way from being the five-dollar man selling songs to performers visiting the penitentiary.

Now in his fifth year of performing for Clement's invited elite, Johnny had learned that any trip to the Mansion could hold a new surprise or opportunity. On one occasion he might be singing for music stars such as Dinah Shore, Tennessee Ernie Ford, or Roy Rogers and Dale Evans, and on another the audience might include political power players such as Senator Lyndon B. Johnson or Senator Albert Gore Sr. But, for the Marigolds, the most noteworthy celebrity experience came on December 21, 1957.

That day, while the quintet was rehearsing in preparation for their performance later at the Governor's Mansion, things on the other side of Nashville were a lot more hectic—Elvis had hit town amidst the two-day-old bombshell that he'd received his draft notice.

Gordon Stoker, of the Jordanaires (the group was based in Nashville, and went on to become Elvis's unofficial backup group for records, TV, film, and often live local performances), remembers the day: "Elvis came to bring [Christmas gifts to] D. J. Fontana, Scotty Moore, the four Jordanaires, and Colonel Parker. The Colonel called me out to his office to pick up the gifts. [That year Elvis had brought the Colonel an $1,800 Isetta sports car.]

"Elvis said to me, 'If I had some dress clothes, I'd go down to the Grand Ole Opry with you guys tonight.' I told him that if he would go with us, I would gladly arrange with a local store for that. He went with me downtown, but to my surprise he picked a complete tux outfit, down to the shoes."

But Elvis did not perform that night, cutting short his Opry visit with just a walk-on and a wave to the audience. He was actually in Nashville for another engagement later that night.

At the time, Elvis, like the Marigolds, was getting lambasted in the press over the special privileges his celebrity status was allowing him. When word got out that Paramount Pictures had convinced the army to delay Elvis's induction so he could finish his next picture, *King Creole,* the media had climbed all over Presley and the armed forces.

Meanwhile, the Marigolds were heading over to the Governor's Mansion. Expecting a long night, the warden sent down word to bring blankets since the prisoners would be staying over. (They occasionally slept over at the governor's request; this time Clement wanted them to accompany him the next morning to the McKendree Methodist Church in downtown Nashville, where Clement would preach and the group would sing.)

Late that afternoon they performed for a few dozen politicians and advisers, using the second-floor sitting room as their very own concert hall. Bob Clement and Johnny remember that the matinee ran from 4:00 P.M. until about 7:00 P.M. Then the group, consisting of Johnny, Al Brooks, Hal Hebb, Willy Wilson, and Henry "Dishrag" Jones, broke for dinner in the kitchen. From the kitchen they could hear the scattered applause coming from the dining room, indicating the speeches were in progress.

By 9:00 P.M. they were back upstairs for another show. According to Bob Clement, that evening's performance was attended by family members only. Still, the governor's residence resounded with a pot-pourri ranging from the Swan Silvertones' "My Rock" to the Marigolds' own hit, "Rollin' Stone."

Around 10:00 P.M. the sound of several cars pulling up the driveway created a buzz through the Mansion. Into the sitting room, followed by an entourage of state troopers, glamour girls, and guards, walked the governor's special guest—Elvis Presley—along with Colonel Parker. Elvis shook hands with Clement, Clement's wife, Lucille, and son Bob, then sat down as the singing group continued to stare in shock.

Johnny had been getting hoarse and his voice was fading, so Hebb moved up front to sing lead. Johnny whispered to Dishrag and the others, "Do that new Elvis thing," and then announced, "In honor of the governor's newest guest, we're gonna do a tribute song."

They launched into, of all things, "Jailhouse Rock" (coincidentally *Billboard*'s number-two record on that day). Before the song ended, Elvis was up and singing. When he and Johnny made eye contact, Elvis smiled and Johnny knew that he remembered their first meeting at Sun Studios.

After the number and the applause ended, Elvis called out, "Good to see you, Johnny." Feeling like an equal for the moment, Johnny proudly called back, "Good to see ya, Presley." After a few more vocal tradeoffs, Elvis sat down at the piano. (According to Ben Weisman, writer of fifty-seven songs recorded by Presley, "Most people didn't realize, because Elvis didn't do it on record or concerts much, but he played a decent piano by ear.")

With five Black voices in harmony behind him, Elvis sang a magical rendition of "Just Walkin' in the Rain." When he topped off the last note with four-part harmony around him, and with Johnny going to falsetto, there was a standing ovation. As the clapping died down, Elvis was apparently heard to say, "That's one of my favorite songs."

The night continued with Elvis and the Marigolds alternating tunes. Johnny, drained physically and emotionally by the excitement of the evening, and his voice fading even more, sat off to the side with Elvis, behind the piano. He remembers the star saying, "Johnny, that guy [Hebb] you have over there's tearing me all to pieces. Him and your group, man, those guys are singing!"

Johnny responded, "Yeah, but you're Presley."

Elvis, ignoring the praise, asked, "You play this dump a lot?"

"Much as I can," Johnny said, then persisted, "What's it like, Presley?"

"Bein' a star? Well, it's the best and the worst of everything."

Johnny responded seriously, "You too, huh."

Elvis, apparently understanding what Johnny meant, said, "You ain't the only prisoner, Johnny. My bars are just different. Still, there's worse ways to live."

"But you're Presley!" Johnny insisted. "How could it be better?"

"I don't know," Elvis said quietly, "sometimes you just want 'em to all leave you alone."

Late night became early morning and the festivities finally ended about 3:00 A.M. The group didn't seem to have a song in their repertoire left unsung. Johnny, standing no more than ten feet away, overheard Presley tell the Colonel, "I'd love to sing with these guys. Can't we get 'em on a session or something?"

Johnny knew it was a wasted wish. "He wanted to sing with us, but they [Parker] wouldn't let 'im. See, back in those days it was the Whites and the niggers, you understand what I'm sayin'? I don't blame 'em, they couldn't take no chance on gettin' hurt."

Bob Clement, who was fourteen at the time and remembers the night vividly, says: "I was mesmerized by Elvis. I'd never seen anyone perform like him. My dad liked him too, and I heard him teasing Colonel Parker about Elvis because Elvis worked on a Tennessee State Highway crew part-time one summer before he was a star. My dad felt that, in effect, Elvis worked for him, and told the Colonel, 'I should have discovered Elvis first!'" (Though Congressman Clement insists his father stated that Elvis worked on a state highway crew, there are no records of his employment as such.)

As word spread inside the penitentiary of the Marigolds' evening with Elvis, Johnny knew he was losing control of the balancing act he had maintained for so long. Every bit of press, every sign of privilege for Bragg was a provocation to other inmates.

Others were feeling the heat too. Johnny was personally closer to Hebb than to the other members of the group, and some convicts told Hal Hebb, in no uncertain terms, to watch his step.

It wasn't long before threats once again turned to violence. Hal and Dishrag were loading laundry when several Whites jumped them and beat them up. One grabbed Hebb and told him his days of privilege were over; they warned him that only if he quit singing might he stay alive. They offered him time to think on it, as they opened a huge washing-machine door, threw him inside, turned it on, and ran away.

Various group members were feeling more and more isolated from the general inmate population and didn't want to be caught in the wrong place at the wrong time. Al Brooks and Willy Wilson were goaded into meaningless fights by jealous cons. The very existence of the group was being tested.

A rehearsal was in progress in the auditorium when L. B. McCollough decided he wasn't in the mood for music. Johnny, who by now considered himself the group's manager (actually, it was his determination that was holding the group together), wasn't taking any guff. He knew that insurrection and slacking off were contagious, and he came down harder than a guard on McCollough. Johnny wasn't subtle and he also wasn't one to back away, even from McCollough who was considerably bigger and stronger. The quarrel very rapidly became personal.

"What's with you, L. B.? You're playin' like a drunk," Johnny said.

L. B. responded like a spoiled kid, "I don't feel like playin'."

Johnny tried the extent of his diplomacy. "We're playin' a county fair tomorrow. The governor's gonna be there. We gotta sound good."

"I'll play when I wanna play," L. B. decided. "You and your buddy the governor'll just have to dance without L. B.'s guitar playin'."

By then Johnny had just about lost it. "You'll play now. And I'll tell ya somethin' else, next gig ain't gonna be no phone calls. You gonna play it straight."

Johnny had upped the ante and McCollough threw a round-house punch, clipping Johnny on the fleshy right side of his face. Johnny wasted no time in equalizing the debate, and rationalized with L. B. the way his prison education had taught him to. He took the guitar and broke it across L. B.'s head.

When the guard outside ran in to check on the disturbance, all he saw were Brooks and Dishrag picking McCollough up off the floor, while Hebb went into a song and dance about how L. B. had slipped off his stool and landed on his guitar. McCollough did play the next day, but with a borrowed instrument.

The prison auditorium and its dressing rooms had been Johnny's bailiwick since his assignment there at the beginning of the decade. Everyone knew it and knew where to find him.

One day Johnny was walking toward the poorly lit backstage area. Automatically, he put out his hand to open the door. An inmate named Curly, who was next to Johnny, knocked his hand away.

As Johnny tells it: "I said, 'What's happenin', Curly?' and he said, 'Don't touch it, you're s'posed to be dead.'"

Curly then kicked in the door, as sparks shot from a light switch attached by bare wires to the inner knob.

"They tried to electrocute me."

Years later an inmate told Johnny how some cons figured that if they got rid of Bragg, the Marigolds would be finished forever. The informer never said who those cons were, and Johnny really didn't want to know.

A few weeks after that incident, Johnny was involved in a more direct confrontation. He entered a stairwell as four inmates were descending. Two passed him, then turned around and pulled out what appeared to be sharpened spoons, though at least one had a knife. A staring contest ensued for what Johnny says seemed like forever. During the long period of silence, several other inmates came down the stairs. The aggressors moved to one side and Johnny moved slowly into step with the others until he was safely out of the stairwell.

He looked over his shoulder as he ran to the courtyard, but the assailants never came out of the doorway. Still, he kept running toward the middle of the west field, stopping only when he felt he was in the farthest open space.

Though Johnny never let on, word did get back to Warden Bomar. Rumblings among the inmates had escalated to the point that something had to be done before the whole prison erupted. The penal system was better served by removing provocation wherever possible. So the warden moved Johnny to the prison farm for day labor.

A 1959 news account in the *Nashville Banner* said, in essence, that by the late 1950s, when he was in the prison, Johnny was constantly in fear for his life. His rise to sudden fame, the large income, and the privileges granted him for personal appearances made him the target of the other convicts' jealousy. The article also stated that he had complained about having to buy protection, and that prison extras such as candy and soft drinks always cost him double.

Johnny denied those reports, but it's not likely the warden and governor were going to let their star protégé become an embarrassment to the program by getting himself killed on their watch. That as much as anything may have been the motivation behind the plan the governor had been hatching for some time. It just wasn't the right moment.

In mid-February 1958, Frank Clement's longtime associate, campaign manager, and commissioner of agriculture, Buford Ellington, formally announced his candidacy for governor. Ellington's secretary since Clement's first run for office in 1952 had been Frank's sister and adviser, Anna Belle Clement.

Denied by law from seeking a second term in office, Clement could not run for governor again until 1962. He endorsed Ellington, but only after a long deliberation that rankled the former Clement ally.

Ellington won the August primary and would sweep aside the Republican competition in the fall. The Democrats were still the power in Tennessee, but the political winds were shifting.

By the early fall of 1958, former Warden Edwards, thanks in part to an endorsement letter from the governor, had since moved on to become the director of personnel at the Ford Motor Company's glass plant located only three hundred yards from the prison. Numerous ex-cons found their way to the assembly line courtesy of Edwards and Clement.

One night during dinner at the Mansion, Edwards remembers talking with Clement about his career. Clement was sure that he would be back as governor, but for the time being he was going back to private law practice. He told Edwards there were still a few things, however, that he wanted to take care of before he left office.

The next morning he had a conversation with Warden Bomar. Bob Clement believes that his father's decision crystallized the following night after he spent time talking with Lucille, telling his wife that Bomar thought Johnny Bragg's time had come.

Clement, too, believed—or wanted to believe—that it was time to let Johnny go. He decided to deliver the good news the following night. He also thought about connecting Johnny with Jack Stapp at Tree Music for a staff writing deal. After all, Johnny wasn't going to have the Penitentiary Booking Agency working for him anymore.

In early December 1958, the Marigolds once more brought their brand of gospel, pop, and rock to the manor. By Clement's standards it was an abbreviated evening, only about an hour of performance and few speeches. The governor picked an appropriate lull toward the evening's end to take Johnny aside.

Bob Clement recalls that, with the group and guests still within earshot, the governor said, "Johnny, you may notice a lot of familiar faces here tonight. All these people have seen you sing here many, many times. Well, I feel it's only fitting they be here tonight especially. This has been a long time coming and I don't mind telling you, I wasn't sure it was ever going to happen. But the parole board has been reviewing your case and I've recommended they commute your sentence. You're gonna be free."

The all-White, well-to-do audience applauded a Black man's anticipated return to society. Johnny tried to hold in his emotions but the shock was obvious. He says his first instinct was to hug the governor, but he quickly remembered who and where he was.

"God bless you, Governor," he just said over and over.

"He already has. Good luck, my friend," Clement said. The governor put out his hand and Johnny shook it with both of his. Clement then put his other hand on top of Johnny's.

Another month passed, the new year began, but still nothing happened. Then on January 16, 1959, in one of Clement's last official acts, he kept his word to the man to whom he'd become so attached. Johnny Bragg was about to go free.

After vacating the Governor's Mansion, Clement and his family resided at their home in Brentwood, Tennessee. The governor's loyal, long-time secretary, Mary Smith, remembers:

"I was called by the governor at his office to bring the commutation papers to his home. It was his last day in office. I arrived about 10:30 in the morning. Johnny Bragg and a guard from the prison were already there. With only the four of us present, the governor signed the pardon [commutation] and said to Johnny, as he put his arm around him, 'I trust you, Johnny. I'm expecting you to go straight.' Johnny was gushing all over. He said, 'You can count on me, Governor. Bless you. Bless you, sir.'"

Afterwards, for ten minutes, Clement led them in prayer.

Newspapers all over the country picked up the story. "I fully believe Johnny is completely rehabilitated," Clement was quoted as saying.

Morale in the prison soared as even the most hardened criminals, and those who had been most jealous of Bragg, felt that if a man with six ninety-nine-year sentences for rape could be set free, then maybe they, too, had a chance to reduce their sentences.

RECORD NO.
9-30917
(107,223)♦
(2:32)

Vocal With
Chorus And
Orchestra

TRUE LOVE WILL NEVER DIE
(Robert Riley)

JOHNNY BRAGG

Johnny, Meet Johnnie

THE PAPERWORK HAD already been done. On the morning of January 28, 1959, the State Pardons and Parole Board met at the West Nashville facility and called before them the prison's most notable inmate.

The meeting lasted only fifteen minutes and their notification was a fait accompli. Johnny had found champions in a governor and two wardens. Even the district attorney who had put him in prison agreed with the commutation of Bragg's sentence.

Johnny left the encounter shaking hands with Warden Bomar and blessing everyone in sight. Bomar said, tongue in cheek, "Stay out of the rain, Johnny," and handed the singer a big black umbrella as a gift.

They walked to the main entrance and exited the prison down the front-office stairs instead of through the usual gate entrance. "I'll tell you one thing," Johnny told Bomar as they stepped outside, "I'll always have witnesses to verify my whereabouts at all times . . . you'll never find me back behind bars again."

The words said in hasty jubilation would be repeated and commented on in the press. As numerous photographers snapped pictures and reporters shouted questions, Johnny could hardly be blamed for his euphoric state.

Condemned to 594 years, he had actually served fifteen years, eight months, and twenty-one days—a bargain if he was guilty, a theft of his youth if he was innocent. But Johnny's career when he lived under lock and key almost certainly offered him better opportunities than he ever would have had in the freedom of the ghetto.

At the time of Bragg's release, as the reporters pressed Bomar for comments, he said, "Johnny Bragg is a natural born entertainer who puts his heart and soul into his work. We all hope he does well."

The official line from the prison noted that Governor Clement's action came *after* the State Pardons and Parole Board recommended the commutation, but the sequence of events was actually the reverse: Clement's late-1958 decision to let Johnny go free was what had instigated the board's recommendation in the first place. The board stated simply, "Bragg has rehabilitated himself sufficiently to return to society."

As photographers continued to flash away, the day's slow drizzle turned into a steady rain. The last original Prisonaire to leave the penitentiary opened his new umbrella and posed for the press on the steps below the stone archway that read Tennessee State Prison.

Johnny's release was a novel piece of news to the White communities of America and a heartwarming ray of hope throughout the African-American enclaves in the dawning days of desegregation.

Johnny moved in with his grandmother Parthenia, a short cab-ride's distance from the prison. His first days at home were filled with calls and letters from well-wishers. And Johnny still seemed to draw the press. In a photo story published soon after his release, the *Nashville Banner* quoted Johnny's assessment that "a year in prison is worth four in college."

He had his suits from the Prisonaires days, some homecooking again, and, more important, about $10,000 in a Nashville Bank. At age thirty-two he also had real freedom of choice about the direction for his life. Music was his obvious choice, but he didn't know exactly what he should pursue.

At first he thought of reassembling the Prisonaires (wanting to call them the Freedomaires), but finding the other four was not easy. Ed Thurman had a job with a moving company and John Drue was back working as a chauffeur.

The only one Johnny ever saw again on the outside was William Stewart. Johnny recalls: "He came to visit me and was so high on drugs that he didn't make any sense."

Since getting the old group back together wasn't going to work out, Johnny next turned to the Ebenezer Missionary Baptist Church in Nashville, where he met three ladies who sang as the Solettes. He began singing with them and soon the new quartet exhibited their skills at churches and local shows.

Johnny's chief mentor, ex-Governor Clement, was still working behind the scenes for him. He introduced the writer/singer to Jack

Stapp, partner with Buddy Killen in Tree Music, and Stapp agreed to sign Johnny as a staff writer. He gave him a $30 advance.

Tree was the same company Robert Riley had been writing for since his release. Their reunion in a writers' room there soon after seems not to have been a memorable moment for Johnny; years later, when he struggled to reconstruct his memories of that meeting, he couldn't remember whether they wrote anything that day. Though he and Riley remained acquaintances and saw one another occasionally after their release, they never did write together after leaving prison.

Johnny used his own tape recorder to take down his ideas. Tree employed people who could learn his compositions, play them by ear, and draft lead sheets from the tape recordings. This meant that Johnny no longer needed to cut percentage deals with scribes and could therefore keep all of his writing royalties. Since his own voice was the best vehicle for his songs, Johnny talked to Stapp about arranging for a new recording deal. That led to an introduction to Decca Records' producer Owen Bradley, and Johnny was subsequently signed to Decca as their first southern R&B artist. He began recording in March of 1959.

To his surprise, R&B was not what Decca had in mind for him. His first solo single and his first record release in three years was "True Love Will Never Die," a typical late '50s, ultra pop, string-laden ballad in a Jackie Wilson/Roy Hamilton style, featuring piano arpeggios. The song was similar to Brook Benton's top-ten hit "It's Just a Matter of Time" and was released in June. According to one newspaper account, the song was backed vocally by the Jordanaires and the recording, with a prominent vocal bass in the bridge, certainly sounds like them. The B side, "Just So That Someone Is Me," was in the same vein but not as strong a song.

One story that never made the press was a visit Johnny received only a few months after his release. According to Johnny, one day a black Cadillac pulled up to Grandma Parthenia's place and out stepped Frank Clement. Quietly making the rounds, he came calling to see how his prize pupil was doing.

Congressman Bob Clement states: "My dad often did things like that—off-the-record encounters to emphasize his concern and help people keep on track."

The meeting had a profound motivational effect on Johnny, who considered the relationship he had with Clement to be a personal one. Seeing the governor was one of the only things he'd missed since gaining his freedom. Johnny told his grandma after the meeting, "That man trusted me to do the right thing in prison. Now he's here to let me know he trusts me to do right outside, and that's what I'm gonna do."

The Solettes and their lead singer parlayed Johnny's visibility into performances in Chattanooga, Memphis, Gallatin, and Atlanta, as well as Nashville. For the time being, Johnny seemed to be on the road back, the road ordained by Clement. But Johnny wasn't prepared for everything he would encounter outside. Whether or not it was paranoia on Johnny's part, he felt that during road trips he was being trailed.

When asked about it years later, he responds: "All I know is that it was security people, like police and things. They were tryin' to see what Johnny Bragg had done and they kept up with us, they followed us everywhere. Governor Clement told me a lot of people didn't like the idea of him lettin' the niggers out of the penitentiary, and his enemies were tryin' to find somethin' they could push back on him to make him look bad."

The first Decca record failed, but another, "Everything's Alright" backed with "World of Make Believe," was released in September.

"Everything" was another Jackie Wilson–styled pop number in a mid-tempo vein and with a characteristic gospel chorus. "World of Make Believe" was a distinct departure from the A side. It was a Conway Twitty–styled, countrified ballad with matching piano riffs in a Floyd Cramer vein and included a female chorus. On September 14 the disc was reviewed by *Billboard,* which thought "World of Make Believe" deserved play and that Johnny handled "Everything's Alright" with zest.

Johnny remembers recording a few other sides about that time, and Gordon Stoker of the Jordanaires confirms: "I believe we did backup to Johnny on a new version of "Just Walkin' in the Rain." Andy McKaie of MCA Records notes that Johnny's session also included a song titled "Have I Stayed Away Too Long," though neither has ever come to light.

During that summer of 1959, Johnny got his long-held wish to play the Grand Ole Opry. He performed solo on a program that included Little Jimmy Dickens and Opry regular Del Wood.

Another Bragg milestone occurred on the heels of his Opry performance. While hanging around at Tree Music he met twenty-three-year-old Texas songwriter, Roger Miller, who was working as a doorman at the Andrew Jackson Hotel. The two songsmiths became fast friends and were together when a call came for Johnny from Bradley's Barn, Owen Bradley's recording studio, telling him that Johnnie Ray was in town. Though Ray had had the hit with "Just Walkin' in the Rain" in 1956, the two had never met and Bradley thought Bragg might like to meet him now.

Johnny remembers, "We [Bragg and Miller] went to the hotel and picked Johnnie up and drove all over town showin' him Nashville. He even met my grandmama and we had a lot of fun."

He says that as they were driving, Ray said to him, "You know, Johnny, your song really gave my career a big lift. I'm glad I got to meet you so I could thank you." Johnny says that he told Ray, "Well, I got your next hit too. Let me know when you're ready."

They stopped at Decca's 16th Avenue Studio where Ray was intending to lay down some tracks. Owen Bradley was there along with some session players, including a young saxophonist, Boots "Yakety Sax" Randolph, who was still four years away from his first hit. Johnny spent a few minutes between tracks singing his newest song, "Laughin' in the Rain," to Ray. Though press photographers were reportedly called to memorialize the moment, no one showed up. As for Johnny and Johnnie, they never saw each other after that night.

Bragg's career got a boost when Robert Riley and Jack Stapp introduced him to a local talent manager, Colonel Manny Taylor, formerly of Russellville, Kentucky, who began booking him into Nashville establishments such as the Del Morocco Club alongside Ray Charles and other notable performers. Johnny sometimes sang backed by the Solettes, sometimes alone with backing musicians.

Taylor even finagled a six-week stand for Johnny in Las Vegas, courtesy of a friend who had an insider's relationship with the owner of the Sands Hotel. Johnny Bragg had hit his high-water mark and, according to the singer, was making as much as $1,000 a week as an opening act for members of the Rat Pack, including Sammy Davis Jr.,

Dean Martin, Peter Lawford, and Frank Sinatra. He also continued working the Chitlin Circuit of small, Black, southern clubs and theaters.

By the end of 1959, nights of visiting clubs and performing, punctuated by days of on-and-off songwriting, had led Johnny back to an unstructured, almost reckless lifestyle. With the structure of prison life in his past, Johnny was making up for lost time—more than fifteen years of lost time—cramming as much fun into his days and nights as possible.

Talking about his times with Roger Miller and other Whites, Johnny says, "We couldn't mix back then, like goin' into clubs and different things, you couldn't eat together in a restaurant, so we ran together. Me and Roger and a bunch of his friends, we did a lotta crazy things . . . take slingshots and knock out the street lights an' stuff like that. We was crazy, y' know, and so we had a lot of fun back in 1959."

Johnny's fun sounded unquestionably like a return to his youth.

Excellorec
Music Co.
BMI

Pop.
Time 2:48

NASHVILLE, TENNESSEE

FOOLISH ME!
(Bragg-Louallen)
JOHNNY BRAGG
45-2078

RECORD CO., 177-3RD AVENUE, N.

Back Again, Five to Ten

A YEAR AND two days after his commutation had been signed by the governor, Johnny Bragg was back in trouble.

On January 18, 1960, at 2:45 A.M., he was arrested after a twenty-year-old blonde woman complained to police. She said that she had pulled over to pick up her purse which had fallen on the car floor, when a Black man approached her and questioned her about a hit-and-run accident. She told police she managed to race off in her car, which had been partially blocked by his car on Gallatin Road. Fifteen minutes later, driving his 1957 salmon-colored Mercury, Johnny was detained and booked.

Johnny said he had been nightclub hopping by himself and had stopped for a red light at Church Street and 13th Avenue when a black car sideswiped his car and sped off. He gave chase, but the black auto eluded him. When he turned north on Gallatin Road near Trinity Lane he noticed a black car parked off the side of the road. He turned around and pulled up alongside, questioned the blonde-haired White woman in the car about the accident, and then he drove off.

A *Nashville Banner* headline that day read, in inch-high type, "Walkin' in Rain Composer Jailed" and included a photograph of three county patrolmen standing over a sitting, solemn-looking Johnny Bragg. "Johnny Bragg, who rocketed to musical fame after writing the yesteryear hit song 'Just Walkin' in the Rain' while still a penitentiary inmate, was arrested and jailed early today after questioning a woman about a hit-and-run accident," the paper trumpeted in its twenty-four paragraph, two-column article.

The *Banner* referred to him as "a short, stocky Negro, who served thirteen [*sic*] years in six rape cases." He was charged with breach of the peace and violation of the state automobile registration law (apparently Bragg had only one license plate on his car, and that plate, on the back, was registered to another car he owned). According to the *Banner*'s account, he "would be questioned later today in several morals cases." They declined to elaborate.

To Johnny it felt like 1943 all over again. He was flung into a lineup, with four different women pointing accusatory fingers. Johnny's attorney Tom Kittrell recalls: "They identified him—now get this—they put him in a lineup with four or five criminals in prison garb and put him up there in his bowler hat, tuxedo, and patent leather shoes. It was like a badge of identification!"

Johnny loved to dress the part of a successful entertainer. But for a Black man to do so in Nashville in that era was an invitation to trouble. When one woman pointed him out, her angry husband drew a pistol on Johnny. As the well-dressed ex-con fled down a corridor, police restrained Bragg's attacker just as he was about to get a shot off. Detectives felt they had an open-and-shut case on their celebrity catch. It boiled down to his word versus four different accusers.

Once again the jury was all White and all male. In Kittrell's opinion: "They were a hard-bitten bunch of jurors. They were more conviction-minded than they are today."

The *Banner* picked up the story two days later with the heading "Been Living Right, Composer Insists."

"What does Johnny Bragg have to say about the latest twists in his rocky road of life?" the newspaper queried, and went on, "Bragg denies the accusations. Other than that, he says very little. Years behind bars, convicts say, teach a man to carefully weigh his every word to lawmen. But what does he say about the accusations? 'I've God as my witness . . . I've nothing to worry about . . . I'm a Christian. I'm not going to get excited about all of this. I've been living right since I got out. I hate the embarrassment, but I know all will be all right eventually. The sheriff's officers have been fair, they'll investigate this whole thing and find out the truth. I've nothing to worry about.'"

On January 23 an Associated Press story stated, "Negro Singer is Indicted," and noted that the "Davidson County grand jury reported two indictments against paroled convict Johnny Bragg on two charges of robbery and attempt to ravish. . . . The State Pardons and Parole Board will meet Wednesday to determine if Bragg violated parole."

A United Press International news account continued the Bragg saga the following day. The wire service reported that "The State Pardons and Parole Board ruled that Johnny Bragg, Negro songwriter and entertainer, was a delinquent parolee. . . . The Board indicated Bragg may be returned to prison even if he is found innocent of the charges against him."

Johnny survived the first round of trials because of timing and Kittrell's penchant for eloquent theatrics. In the first case a woman accused Johnny of beating, choking, and robbing her of $6. As Kittrell recollects: "This woman's being assaulted when he [Bragg] was actually singing in a church in Gallatin, Tennessee, at that exact moment. We had nineteen or twenty choirgirls [as witnesses] and I just ran one after another after another onto the stand, and finally the judge got mad.

"'All this is cumulative,' he said. 'Maybe,' I said, 'but I want it in evidence. I'm entitled to have these witnesses come in and testify. I don't care if it takes ten years, I'm gonna try this case like I think it oughta be tried.' I quoted the Magna Carta, made this big grandstand argument. 'Here's a man standing in the church, doing the Lord's work, and they're accusing him of horrible things, just because he had a bad record.' Of course, he didn't take the witness stand. I couldn't afford to put him on with three to four past convictions."

One newspaper account stated, however, that at least in that particular case, "Bragg had testified that before Monday he 'never saw' the White woman who accused him of attacking her." They also noted the case had gone to the jury that day and if convicted he could get a maximum term of fifty-five years.

Johnny won that trial and the next two in similar fashion. His next accuser, an expectant mother, said he came into her home but left after she pleaded for her unborn child's life. In the third case a woman claimed she was in a basement garage when Johnny supposedly accosted her, only to flee when she screamed. In both of these cases he had been miles away.

Kittrell notes, however, "Johnny was his own worst enemy. They [the police] would pull him over at every stoplight and give him a hard way to go because, hell, ya don't see a Black man in that kinda car, with a bowler hat, every day."

The fourth case was the sideswiping incident. The woman claimed that Johnny attacked her and robbed her of $2.50. Johnny was at a disadvantage in this trial since he had no alibi, and after three losses the prosecutor was anxious to get on the scoreboard with something. Years later even his attorney says, "I really don't know if he did it or not."

Considering the way he dressed, the flashy convertible he drove, and his delight in carrying and flashing big bills, attacking someone for $2.50 made no sense at all. The result of that trial was a hung jury, made up of eleven White men and one Black man, so the prosecutor started over and tried him again. This time the prosecution used FBI paint analysis of the scrapings from the two cars and concluded that the paint could possibly have come from Johnny's car, reportedly one of only five salmon-colored Mercurys in the entire state. On January 28, Johnny was found guilty.

Kittrell says about his client: "He was as sharp as he could be. He acted dumb, but he knew exactly what was going on."

Johnny's lawyer wanted to take the case to the state supreme court, but he was talked out of that by his client. Johnny had been reached through somebody in the penal system who didn't want anyone digging into what had happened to Johnny's money (an undisclosed amount that had disappeared from his penitentiary account). Johnny was told he would be incarcerated no more than six months if he would drop the appeal.

And so he did. But the behind-the-scenes maneuver didn't pay off for Johnny. He was returned for a second round with the prison system. His sentence was five to ten years.

Johnny really believed it couldn't happen, yet there he was, back. It was an event with repercussions. Many inmates hoping for parole told him that their chances for early retirement from state services were ruined when such a celebrated ex-con was once again arrested. They knew that parole board members, politicians, newspaper editors would draw the conclusion that if an apparently successful and trustworthy ex-con couldn't be trusted on the outside, then no one would trust these inmates either.

Johnny, regardless of his guilt or innocence, seemed to Warden Bomar to be one of those men who could handle the structure of prison life better than the disorganization of freedom. He was a model prisoner but seemed to be a failed parolee, and the new governor, Buford Ellington, also knew it.

Johnny realized there was little chance for early parole and he became withdrawn. "I was angry. I got a raw deal, bein' sent back for stealin' $2.50. I never even saw that woman, it was some other guy," he says.

When Ernie Young of Excello Records came to the prison, Johnny turned him away, saying, "I don't wanna record, I don't wanna do nothin'." He said the same to music publisher Red Wortham and even to Buddy Killen of Tree Music, both of whom came out to help Johnny get a new record deal.

So it was just another blow to Johnny's pride when he received notice from Decca Records in February that the label had dropped him for nondeliverance. His contract called for eight recorded sides but up to that point he had only delivered six.

The Visit

chapter eighteen

BUT JOHNNY BRAGG was not for-
gotten. Not long after his reincarceration, attorney Robert S. Clement
(Frank's father) came to the prison with reassurances that Johnny was
in the prayers of the ex-governor and that they would help Johnny's
solicitor Tom Kittrell in any way they could.

Whatever they may have tried neither shortened his stay nor
exonerated him of the $2.50 robbery charge. But it didn't stop Johnny
from believing in help from above.

On March 8, 1961, a rumor went through the prison that someone
important was visiting and it wasn't an official or a politician. Johnny

Bragg was in his cell, as were all the inmates, because of a recent near riot that had resulted in a lockdown. Suddenly a guard ran into the block and went directly to Johnny's cell.

"Warden wants ya, Bragg. You got a visitor out there," he puffed.

As they walked out past the row of cells, Johnny asked who his visitor was. The guard, trying not to smile about the seeming absurdity of his answer because he didn't believe it himself, said, "Elvis Presley's out there."

When they entered the light of the courtyard, there with the warden and the director of state industries was, truly, Elvis Presley and three members of his entourage, along with state police, and several prison guards.

Presley had been in Nashville to accept an award from the joint convention of the Tennessee legislature for his musical achievements as well as for his importance to the state of Tennessee. Though he normally received $50,000 an appearance at that time, Elvis did a guest shot at the legislature for free. In addition to the dignitaries and their families, the capitol galleries overflowed with young truants from school.

According to an article in the *Nashville Banner,* Governor Ellington quipped to the packed house, "With Elvis around, I feel just like I ain't nothing but a hound dog." He then named Elvis a colonel on the governor's staff, complete with certificate.

Elvis, wearing a black suit, white shirt, and black tie, earned a laugh with his opening remark, "Governor Ellington, members of the legislature, and those who skipped school."

He was also heavily applauded when he mentioned, "People frequently want to know if I plan to settle down eventually in Hollywood. Now, I like to go out there to play [laughter], er, work, but my home is in Memphis, Tennessee, and that's where it's going to be." In a more serious moment he said, "This is the finest honor I have ever received."

According to the article, Presley spoke for about five minutes, until a little after 11:00 A.M., and then left for Memphis with his three bodyguards/friends, Joe Esposito, Alan Fortas, and Sonny West.

A small, nearly buried account in a Memphis newspaper stated: "It was Elvis's idea to drive by the penitentiary, one of his traveling companions said. He has known Bragg from back when he was starting out as an entertainer, scrounging for a living."

Johnny recollects that he'd greeted Elvis with, "Presley! What are you doin' in these parts?"

Elvis responded, "Heard you had some trouble. Thought I'd drop by, kinda check up on you."

They didn't shake hands but gravitated to the nearest wall. The circle of entranced spectators created an unofficial and silent perimeter some fifty feet from them. Elvis, still in his legislature attire, smiled a low-key smile as Johnny spoke: "I'm doin' okay, but look at you—fine clothes, big limousine, those pretty girls all over ya!"

They talked some more and Elvis said he wanted to get Johnny a lawyer. Johnny told him he already had a lawyer but he appreciated the offer.

Elvis said, "I know you're a proud man, Johnny, but I'll bet my lawyers can help shorten your time."

Johnny told him that only God and the governor could do that, but neither seemed inclined at the moment. "Well, let me do *something* for you, Johnny. Do you need any money?"

"No, everythin' is fine right now. Governor Clement's helpin' me and his daddy's gonna help me."

Elvis, who was a helping hand to many, kept looking for a way to assist Johnny. "Well, you know, I'm planning on recording 'Just Walkin' in the Rain.' That'll help some more royalties come in."

"Presley," Johnny said, "you don't have to do that. Me and you's good friends, we go way back to when you were a kid in Memphis. I'm fine. You look after Presley. Hell, I sing as much as you and spend a lot less."

After a few more minutes of conversation, they shook hands hard, one on top of another until all four hands were intertwined, and said their goodbyes.

Johnny perceived himself to be an equal of big-time entertainers and he represented himself as such. He had the pride and the self-reliance that goes with the territory. Johnny in his own mind was free and he was *somebody*, no matter what his apparent circumstances.

The guard walked over only after Elvis had returned to the car, where the warden waited. Johnny says he overheard the warden ask, "Anything else you'd care to see, Mr. Presley?"

"Thank you very much," Presley answered, "I've seen who I came to see."

Their meeting had lasted all of ten to fifteen minutes, but it had to have been a tremendous encouragement to Johnny.

Regardless, a fear of being back out on the streets would later begin to insinuate itself into Johnny's thinking. He would believe that being free would only be a prelude to being arrested and recon-fined by Clement's enemies.

Occasional visits to the prison by Roger Miller and Marty Robbins perked up Johnny's often-low spirits. He might have felt even better had he known that Elvis continued to tell friend Jerry Shilling and others, on numerous occasions, that "Just Walkin' in the Rain" was one of his favorite songs.

Shilling says, "He [Elvis] often sang it around the house or wherever when he was feeling blue." Elvis's interpretation of "Just Walkin'" was not that of Johnnie Ray's, but of Johnny Bragg's. Much of Bragg's vocal style can be heard in the way Elvis slides up to a very pure high tenor on songs like "Jesus Knows What I Need."

When I asked Shilling why Elvis never recorded "Just Walkin' in the Rain," he said, "I guess he felt nobody could do it better."

It was not until mid-year that Johnny felt the need to sing again. A show featuring Marty Robbins, Bobby Day, LaVern Baker, and the Harlem Globetrotters had been scheduled at the prison. Everyone had been looking forward to it for a week. At the last minute the chaplain, having been rebuffed several times, tentatively asked Johnny again if he'd care to sing. Johnny liked the idea of being in the company of LaVern Baker and said yes. He soloed with just a piano accompaniment and later admitted to himself that it felt good to be back on stage.

It also felt good to have the leader of the Globetrotters, Meadowlark Lemon, approach him after the show for some songwriting tips. Lemon knew as much about writing as Johnny did about a full court press, but that didn't stop the basketball star from wanting to write. They spent about half an hour together and even began fashioning a song in the dressing room.

Singing and composing reinvigorated Johnny musically, and it helped him break out of the oppressive boredom he had been feeling. He took action and formed yet another Prisonaires, with holdover Alfred Brooks and newcomers Acie Horton, James Doyle, Sullivan Hayes, and Clarence "Two Flats" McKeel on guitar. McKeel was Johnny's contribution to racial progress; he was White.

They practiced in the auditorium, and soon churches, county fairs, schools, and the occasional obligatory Mansion visits became the new group's Chitlin Circuit. Both Warden Bomar and Governor Ellington were delighted that Johnny had ended his self-imposed silence.

The growth of the group could be measured by more than an increase in their repertoire. The music and the experience were changing the men themselves.

Singing in and out of the penitentiary kept Johnny occupied through the following months, and he needed the diversion. The Sunday services were less meaningful for him now than in his first term, and in 1961 his goals had become hazy. But the church service on December 11 provided a critical moment of spiritual reinforcement.

The Jordanaires, who a little over a year before had been singing background for Johnny in the confines of a studio, were back playing the penitentiary just as they had a decade before. The new prison chaplain had arranged for their return. Since attendance for services was voluntary, the Prisonaires were heartened upon seeing the auditorium filled with more than eleven hundred inmates.

"We're glad to be singing," Johnny said, and moments later a hush came over the huge audience as they sang "Silent Night."

The Jordanaires soon followed, to a standing ovation, and applause continued throughout their five spirituals and three hymns. Technically and melodically perfect, the Jordanaires' mellowness communicated their faith through song.

Johnny felt it and so did the other Prisonaires. Johnny says that he and the other members of the group were spiritually renewed by the performance. They wanted their singing to be more than a pastime and an escape. Their objective was now clearly defined:

they would sing their way to freedom, just as Johnny had done before.

During 1962 Johnny began receiving new royalties, thanks to additional recordings of "Just Walkin' in the Rain" by the Ray Conniff Orchestra and by country music legend Jim Reeves. The Prisonaires' road to the Governor's Mansion was also being repaved by the return of Johnny's old supporter.

Frank Clement was once again in the political arena, having announced his candidacy for governor on February 28 at his law office in the Third National Bank Building in Nashville.

When Clement had left the governorship in 1959, he was five months shy of his thirty-ninth birthday. Reluctant to leave politics, the love of his life, but still needing to earn a living, his interim pursuit had become representing insurance firms, securities dealers, and country music artists by way of his own law firm. But throughout those years in private law practice, Clement had often felt melancholy as he longed for the thrills that came with public service.

Again his wife, Lucille, dutifully made appearances to support Frank's ambitions, but the long barnstorming trips and the problems of rearing her sons amidst the pandemonium of political life became increasingly difficult for her. Nevertheless, when he announced his campaign for a third term in office, Lucille, Anna Belle, and the governor's three sons were all there with him to lend support.

Clement handily defeated his Democratic party rival in the August primary election, and in the fall of 1962, running on his record of accomplishment in education, highway development, and the area of mental health, Frank Clement was reelected to the state's top position (a job that now paid $18,500 a year).

Though his victory was by more than 112,000 votes, the comparatively large numbers run up by his Republican party and Independent party opponents indicated that the tide was starting to turn against Tennessee Democrats.

The governor's ambitions still included a hope for national political prominence, and on August 10, 1963, only eight months into his new term, he again felt the lure of higher office when Senator Estes Kefauver died.

Realizing his constituents would not take kindly to a new governor abandoning them for the U.S. Senate so soon after being elected, Clement named longtime loyalist and aging state legislator Herbert "Hub" Walters to fill Kefauver's Senate seat until the next regular election in 1964.

In those days Clement was greatly comforted by the fact that his dear sister had agreed to take a position in his cabinet as administrative assistant. Though Anna Belle Clement had been his unofficial political right arm in his first two terms, she gained a greater authority in this present term. As the governor became preoccupied with plans for the 1964 Senate run, Anna Belle became the power behind the throne as the chief of staff and dispenser of patronage from her small office on the lower floor of the capitol building.

In effect, she was the most powerful woman in the state. Miss Anna Belle, as everyone called her, was a well-connected and talented politician who had all the charm that her brother had. At five feet nine inches tall, slender, and with two-inch heels and piled-high hair, she was an imposing and, as many had learned, strong-willed figure. Her nephew Bob Clement once noted with apparent pride, "She can cut you into small pieces and you'll walk away feeling like a million dollars."

"Frank called my job 'AA,' which I took to mean administrative assistant, until one day when he was going out of town for a while and he told me it also meant 'always available' and that's what he expected me to be," Anna Belle says laughingly. "Of course, he could overrule things I decided to do, but I was for all intents and purposes his decision-maker."

It turned out that one decision Anna Belle made saved Johnny Bragg's life. Johnny had been due to perform one afternoon, but came down with food poisoning and was taken to the prison hospital in extremely serious condition. When the warden called Miss Anna Belle, she took it upon herself to authorize Johnny's immediate removal to Nashville's Baptist Hospital. He recovered two days later.

"I was happy to see my efforts help Johnny survive," the stateswoman recalls. "In all the time I knew him I always felt he regretted the path he took, but in prison he had found the Lord and peace in his heart. He certainly couldn't have sung with that kind of conviction without a strong belief in God. I found him to be tranquil, with no bitterness."

Johnny was such a fixture around the Mansion that he developed warm relationships with the members of Clement's family. The governor's son Bob fondly remembers their encounters. "Johnny and I spoke often, mostly in the kitchen. We talked about many things—religion, music, singers he'd performed with. I loved Johnny. He was so personable, no doubt he was the leader of the group. He was an electrifying performer. I liked him from the first day I ever met him. I just thought of him as my friend. He was always polite, respectful, appreciative, but enthusiastic and in good spirits . . . and he seemed to be very repentant."

Frank Clement's term became heavily occupied with legislation, including the establishment of a statewide system of vocational training schools, a state-sponsored student loan program, and increases in welfare benefits. But Clement's genuinely progressive reforms were slowed by allegations (never proven) of a partnership with well-known wheeler-dealer Billie Sol Estes.

(Estes, reportedly a friend of President Lyndon Johnson's, was convicted less than two years later and sentenced to fifteen years in prison for selling $35-million worth of nonexistent fertilizer tanks. Adding to Estes's seedy image, he reportedly testified before a grand jury that he was present at a meeting in which President Johnson ordered the killing of an agricultural department official.)

With so much else on his political agenda, Clement was not able to champion the cause of prison reform as visibly as before. Of course, it did not stop him from entertaining as before, and the Prisonaires were once again able to meet the elite.

Anna Belle remembers: "Guests at those soirees included, among many others, Eddy Arnold [whose 1948 number-one hit, "Anytime," was the governor's favorite pop song], Minnie Pearl, Johnny Cash, June Carter Cash, and the ever present Billy Graham."

Johnny tells the story that among the multitude one evening was Alabama governor George Wallace, who said upon hearing the group sing, "You boys are a great credit to your race of people."

According to Johnny, Wallace also said, "I've been rapped at being a great segregationist and if I hadn't been rapped that way I never would have been governor, but I didn't hate Black people. Some of my best friends are Black people, but in order to be governor down here you gotta act like you hate Black people or you won't be able to be governor." It put into perspective Clement's amazing success in befriending and sponsoring Johnny Bragg and the Prisonaires.

When the time came in 1964 for the U.S. Senate primary race, Clement ran against challenger Ross Bass. Tennesseans may have felt a kinship for Clement as governor, but they were apparently not ready to send him to Washington. Bass sent Clement back to full-time stewardship of the governor's office by a plurality of almost 100,000 votes and went on to defeat Republican Howard Baker Jr. in the fall.

On May 5, 1965, there was a bittersweet reunion in the prison when Johnny noticed a familiar face at the mess hall. Marcel Sanders was back. He'd been sentenced to one to three years for burglarizing a service station with three friends, each having absconded with a car battery.

Johnny was glad to see him but was sorry Marcel had crossed the line again. The sorrow was momentary, however, as Sanders' solid bass voice was redrafted into the Prisonaires. The group now consisted of two original Prisonaires, Bragg and Sanders; one Marigold, Brooks; and the three relatively new Prisonaires, Horton, Hayes, and Doyle on guitar.

By early summer Johnny had voluntarily loosened his usually tight grip on the group by shortening rehearsals and sometimes eliminating them altogether. He was preoccupied with thoughts of getting out of his five-to-ten-year sentence. A new hearing was coming his way.

On July 27 he went before the parole board. His sister, step-mother, and a local minister appeared before the board in his support. His chances looked good, but he didn't know that outside forces were once again dictating his destiny.

Twelve days earlier an eleven-year-old girl had been raped and murdered while she was babysitting. State commissioner Harry Avery asked Johnny, "What would have happened if you had been out on parole when the rape occurred?" Johnny was merely stating facts when he said, "I would probably have been immediately questioned." It was too cynical for the board. They denied Johnny parole.

On the basis of the board's decision, it could be said that since there would always be rapes, and Johnny would always be a suspect, he should never be let out. It was beginning to look as though that's the way it would be, as others were once again being released ahead of him. Months turned into years and still Johnny was left to serve out his time. In February 1967 Marcel Sanders was paroled for what would be his last time. More than ever, Johnny prayed that some way would be found to set him free.

What became famous in Tennessee as the "leapfrog government" had taken another jump in late 1966 when the former governor, Buford Ellington, again won the state's highest office. Ellington took over from Governor Clement, who had evened the score with Ross Bass by besting him for the Democratic nomination for Senate candidate. But in the general election Clement lost to Republican Howard Baker Jr.

Clement's loss to Baker by almost 100,000 votes had been a devastating blow. It left him with nowhere to go politically. He once again returned to the practice of law. His life was in turmoil. Though during his career Clement had won four of six elections, including a primary, and had never been defeated for the post of governor, his future in politics was in doubt.

Anna Belle recalls other concerns of the emotional ex-governor: "His wife was sick during this time and I truly feel he was a very lonely man. Frank Clement had some hurts on the inside that he couldn't talk to us about."

There was little "the mighty, mighty man" could do for Johnny these days, but a chance meeting with Woodlawn Cemetery owner H. Raymond Liggon gave him an idea.

At the McKendree Methodist Church, after one of Clement's fire-and-brimstone sermons, Liggon mentioned to Clement how much he enjoyed the services and specifically the uplifting singing of the man from prison. He had heard Johnny sing several times at the church.

The ex-governor told Liggon that the sooner Johnny could get a sponsor and find work, the sooner he could put his talent to use beyond the prison walls. Liggon offered to give Johnny some work at the cemetery. He believed Johnny's vocalizing would be a proper send-off for any mortal.

Excellorec
Music Co.
BMI

R&B
(Novelty) Vocal
Time 2:49

"PORK AND BEANS"
(J. Bragg)
THE SOLOTONES
45-2060 A
177-3RD AVENUE, N.

Mentor No More

THE LAND MASS of Tennessee is 41,797 square miles, of which a six-by-eight-foot portion had belonged to John Henry Bragg for twenty-four of the last twenty-five years.

On November 3, 1967, Johnny Bragg was once again paroled to his sister, Dorothy, in Nashville to start a new life. He went to work for Reverend Raymond Liggon at Woodlawn Cemetery, singing at the gravesites during funeral ceremonies and cleaning up around the mortuary. Occasionally he dug and filled in plots.

Johnny relates another remarkable story of celebrity contact. The story can't be proven; it sounds particularly improbable. But the life of Johnny Bragg is a study in improbability, so perhaps Johnny should be believed about this encounter too.

Despite being paroled to his sister, he stayed down the road at Grandma Parthenia's place and it was there, on a Wednesday Johnny insists, that he had an unexpected visitor. Arriving on a motorcycle and wearing a black leather jacket was Elvis. How he found Johnny isn't explained, though it obviously would not have been hard for a person with Presley's connections to find almost anyone.

Johnny says: "Elvis was upset. He was different now, he wasn't funny now, he didn't smile. He said he was upset with all the people around him at Graceland who were spongin' offa him. Elvis was the type a man that he wanted to help everybody. He was just that type a guy, but he was different now. I thought he mighta been high when he visited. Elvis came in packin' a big ol' pistol on his side, and said 'Johnny, I wanna get me a nap, and when I wake up we're gonna talk.'"

After Elvis awoke, Johnny recalls, "he sat down at Grandma Parthenia's ol'-time [player] piano and played 'It Is No Secret What God Can Do.'" He says that Elvis seemed to take solace in the down-home setting, while singing the soothing spiritual and chording away on the rickety piano.

After a few innocuous exchanges, Johnny says Elvis got up to leave and he walked him to the door.

"What's eatin' you, Presley?" he asked.

"I just feel like shootin' all the motherfuckers at the mansion [Graceland] who get on my nerves," Presley said, according to Johnny's recollection. Elvis wasn't specific and he didn't elaborate further. He walked out of the house, got on his motorcycle, and roared away. He was gone as quickly as he arrived. No long goodbyes, just a quick "see ya, Johnny." But neither ever saw the other again.

When Frank Clement had introduced Johnny to Reverend Liggon at the time of Johnny's parole, it was the last of many good services that Clement performed for Bragg.

In 1968 Liggon and his associate Sewell Jackson had an idea. They felt that Johnny's talent should again be heard by a larger public and they wanted to start a record label. They told him that they would put up the money and provide an office, and Johnny would write and sing the songs.

Liggon said, "We've even got a name for it—L for Liggon, B for Bragg, and J for Jackson—Elbejay Records." They made a handpainted, two-foot-long sign displaying the name and hung it above the door.

The office was located in the basement between the embalming room and the gravesite sales office of the funeral home—a bizarre place indeed to find a one-room record company.

Johnny used his Elbejay office for hours at a time, creating lyrics and melodies for new songs he hoped to record. He worked at an old, wooden flattop desk, bare except for some pencils, a pad, and a Wollensak reel-to-reel tape recorder. There was an elderly upright piano, his World War II–vintage Webcor radio, and a few decaying chairs. The windowless, dirty white walls were covered with framed old photos and a few faded press clippings. Above the desk was a picture, at least fifteen years old, of Bragg, grinning for the camera, standing side by side with Frank Clement in the governor's office.

A guitar player, Skippy White, came in from time to time to put Johnny's newest ideas on sheet music and play along behind him.

In short order Johnny wrote several new compositions and picked two, "They're Talkin' About Me" and "Is It True?" as the debut recordings. "Talkin'" was an up-tempo, Motown-styled rocker with an insistent bass-and-drum rhythm. If the Supremes had ever sung backup for a soulful male lead, it might have sounded like Johnny and his backup group did on that record. Between Bragg's vocal maturity, his stylized confidence, and the advancement in recording technology, his new track featured him as a contemporary soul artist with vocal power aplenty.

The B side, "Is It True?" was a melodic, soul/rhythm ballad that built with each verse, adding Muscle Shoals–styled horns and girl-group backing. Bragg's baritone-to-falsetto wailing was assured and exciting. He might not have succeeded in the mainstream R&B marketplace, but he certainly sounded like he belonged there.

Johnny remembers: "I had different backup people. We used a lot of people from Decca Records and some of Owen Bradley's people too." He recorded the sides at Bradley's studio on February 3, 1969, and after ten long years was finally back in the record business.

When Liggon suggested they hire a promotion man, Johnny used the time-honored method of many '50s Black artists who were cheated yet kept going back for more; for these artists, so resigned to being ripped off, it must have seemed true that the devil you know is better than the devil you don't. He hired Red Wortham, and claimed Red was so thankful for the job that he owned up to what Johnny had suspected all along.

"I asked Red, 'I thought Sam Phillips got all the money?' He said, 'No, Johnny, I'm just gonna tell you the truth. I did it, I'm not gonna lie to you, and I appreciate you gettin' me out here to help these people with the record company. If you just forgive me for what I did, I'll make it up some kinda way.'"

Johnny said, "I have a lot of respect for you for tellin' the truth. Everybody makes mistakes, I've made mistakes, and I'm gonna make some more."

Elbejay's first release came and went with little notice outside of Tennessee, though six years later a reissue in England of "They're Talkin' About Me," sporting a multicolored picture sleeve, became a popular item among record collectors of northern soul, a regional style of soul music emanating from artists usually recording in cities like Detroit, Chicago, and Cleveland.

Meanwhile, Johnny kept on composing, performing, and working his day job at the cemetery. One of his bookings led him to a club in Knoxville, Tennessee. After his performance he met Gail Green, a good-looking, twenty-nine-year-old woman from Melville, Tennessee, a small town north of Knoxville.

Gail fell in love with his singing, his songs, and his sincerity. And Johnny, who had seen enough trouble in his life, had now fallen in love with a White woman in the South (though Gail's father was Cherokee, she looked somewhat Caucasian). Gail's parents owned a dairy and were well-to-do, according to what she told Johnny. Despite her parents' own mixed marriage, when word of Gail's new boyfriend reached them it was apparently her mother who stated, "We don't want no nigger in this family!"

In spite of the social animosity felt toward them, Gail and Johnny's relationship blossomed. They met frequently in Nashville while she still lived at home with her parents across the state. After a particularly romantic evening together, Gail abruptly and surprisingly told Johnny she had to leave. Weeks passed and no one, not even Johnny, knew if she had gone to sort out her feelings or sort out her family life. Three weeks later Gail showed up at Johnny's apartment carrying a suitcase and a .22-caliber rifle, and announced that she was moving in.

"I brought you the gun cuz in this town you need protection," she said, then she opened the suitcase. Johnny's eyes nearly left their sockets. Piled on top of several layers of clothing were stacks of hundred-dollar bills, amounting to about $15,000—money of her own or from a family trust, apparently. One might call it her unofficial dowry; Johnny never asked where it came from.

On Tuesday evening, November 4, 1969, at approximately seven o'clock, Frank Clement was driving to a dinner at the home of his personal lawyer and old friend, David Alexander. He never arrived.

His car veered into another lane and smashed head-on into another car on Franklin Road. He was killed instantly, suffering massive chest injuries, seventeen years to the day after being elected governor for the first time.

His body was taken to General Hospital. With Lucille hospitalized in Virginia (she had voluntarily entered a facility for help with depression), son Bob in the army at Fort Gordon, and Frank Jr. at Memphis State University, it was left up to his youngest son, James Gary Clement, to identify the body of his departed dad. Later that evening, under instructions from the ex-governor's father, Robert S. Clement, Frank's body was brought to his hometown of Dickson.

Alexander was likely the last person to have spoken with Clement. He was representing Frank in a divorce suit that Lucille had filed earlier in the year, though Alexander had felt there was still an opportunity for reconciliation.

The news came to Johnny over the radio. He was devastated. Governor Clement, a towering soul of invincibility, had been his friend, his guiding angel who gave direction and hope. Now, Johnny thought, the governor was with the angels himself. He felt that there was essentially no way for him to express his gratitude or his grief, except to pray for Frank G. Clement's soul.

And sing at his funeral.

I'M FREE
THE PRISONER'S SONG
(Johnny Bragg)

Publisher:
ELBEJAY
Nar
Se. ill   n
Bl-il
Time: J:20

105   JOHNNY BRAGG

ELBEJAY Enterprises, Inc.; P. O. Box 8905, Nashville, Tennessee 37211

"I Think Johnny Bragg Has Suffered Enough"

chapter twenty

FOLLOWING FRANK CLEMENT'S death, Johnny went into a serious depression.

His new 45, "I'm Free," faded into instant obscurity. It was his thirteenth released single and the last of his career. The recording, with a forty-eight-second spoken introduction by the deep-voiced Sewell Jackson telling of Johnny's life as a convict, was a heartwrenching, melancholy, gospel/blues ballad that summarized Johnny's struggle. But accompanied only by guitar, the recording itself sounded like it was done on a home tape recorder in the very mortuary basement where he wrote it.

The flip side, "Hurt And Lonely," was a full-blown, horn-laden, blues ballad with a gospel-styled female group backing Johnny's extraordinary vocal gyrating and classic soul wailing that would have impressed the likes of Wilson Pickett and Otis Redding. The record deserved a better fate but, in essence, Elbejay was a record company in name only, without the financial resources and knowledge to get and maintain radio's attention.

With his longtime mentor dead, Johnny would soon begin to feel that the forces allied against Clement would not stop their prejudices toward him just because their adversary was gone.

On December 14, 1969, Johnny was out driving with a friend, Billy Brown, on Murfreesboro Road. Brown stopped to pick up a fine-looking female dressed in hooker attire, who was flagging them down. Johnny claimed he wanted no part of the girl who asked if they wanted to have a good time. But Billy was game and the girl climbed in. Before he could even shift gears, several policemen also climbed in.

She was, according to Johnny, a setup, and he and Billy were taken to the Nashville lockup. Johnny was booked for aiding and abetting prostitution. He was held in the county jail until January 17, 1970, when he was sent back to the Tennessee State Prison for the third time. Gail's visits were all that sustained him.

Then, on February 4, the parole board granted Johnny a third parole, though it took the system until May 12 to release him into the custody of Ray Liggon. Johnny quickly immersed himself in writing for Elbejay and began acquiring songs from other cons and ex-cons, in hopes of helping their rehabilitation (and making them money) through music.

Johnny and Gail's love affair entered a new phase after she became pregnant in April 1971. By Christmas time, she was awaiting birth at Maharry Hospital, Nashville's "Blacks only" medical facility, when the couple decided to get married.

Not knowing that his sister, upon hearing the news, was arranging for a reverend to come to the hospital, Johnny had taken Gail out of her hospital bed, got her into and out of a cab, and then up the courthouse steps to the clerk's office.

Johnny recalls: "There was a Black lady with us which was a good friend of my wife and we was talkin' on the line at the court, and the man said, 'You all come on up here now if you're gonna get married, cuz we ain't got all day. Come on up here!' And the Black woman looked at the ol' man and she said, 'It's not me—it's her!'"

Johnny says that when the clerk looked to where the woman was indicating, and saw that Gail was White, he opened his mouth so wide that his false teeth fell out onto the desk. After he noticed Gail's delicate condition he regained his composure, picked up his teeth, and stammered, "We ain't got all day? We ain't got all of a *minute!*" And the fastest marriage ceremony in Nashville history was on the books.

After the three rushed back to the hospital, they found that a religious version of the ceremony was about to be presided over by a Reverend Moody. Johnny's sister, Dorothy, and brother James attended, along with a score of nurses, as Johnny and Gail exchanged vows for a second time, this time a religious bedside ceremony, on that Tuesday, December 28. Two days later, Misti Bragg was born to the newly wedded couple.

A mixed marriage in the South was a constant provocation to authorities. One summer day when Gail and Johnny went swimming at Hermitage Landing, they had no idea how much danger they were courting.

Wearing just their bathing suits, they drove from the landing to a local lover's lane. "Everybody sat and listened to music, sat in their cars, and police drove up and said, 'I got Johnny Bragg! I got him! Everybody out of the car! He's in the car with a naked White woman!' She had her swimmin' suit on an' I had my swimmin' trunks on," Johnny recalls. "Some of the police officers say they didn't want no part of it. They said it was one of the other cops, he wanted his name in the paper. One cop ranted, 'You want some White meat, huh boy? That Bible-totin' governor turned you loose, but I got you now!'"

When Gail protested that she was his wife, the peace officer said, "Yeah, and I'm Martin Luther King!" Johnny and Gail were whisked downtown and put through the humiliation of a booking. Though they were soon released, Gail was now seeing firsthand some of what Johnny had been living with for decades.

The ghost of Johnny's notoriety reared its head again in November 1974, when a nineteen-year-old female, arrested for robbery, claimed to have been picked up by a man she later identified from a few chosen photos as Bragg. She claimed that he had given her a blank pistol and a holdup note that she used to rob a liquor store.

Johnny vehemently denied the charge and agreed to submit to a lie detector test. He passed. Additionally, his teenaged accuser hadn't known that the man she chose couldn't read or write, so there went the holdup-note theory. Still, the police had spent the taxpayers' time and money trying to pin Johnny as the mastermind, though there's some reason to think that the accusation was painstakingly contrived; a month had passed between the incident and Bragg's arrest.

But this time the evidence was even too flimsy for the racists. In his long bout of life's conflicts, at least that round went to Johnny Bragg.

The next round didn't go as well. On an April afternoon in 1977, Johnny, Gail, and Misti stopped at a store on Dickerson Road, bought some groceries, and, as Johnny paid, Gail and Misti went to the car. As Johnny left the store he saw a White man in sneakers, a yellow windbreaker, and blue jeans, shouting at Gail while pushing and shoving her against their car.

Johnny dropped the bags and ran toward them, confronting what he considered to be an intoxicated thief. The man pulled a gun, but in an instantaneous scuffle Johnny disarmed him. The presumed rummy yelled, "I'm a cop!" Johnny said, "I think you're a wino," and threw the gun in the bushes after pushing aside what he perceived to be a drunken purse-snatcher.

The Bragg family drove off. Johnny was livid that someone should accost his wife. "Imagine that bastard sayin' he was a cop," Johnny fumed. "He was a cop. I know him," Gail timidly volunteered. "His name's Gary. I had dinner with him a few times, long ago. Please don't be angry," she said. Johnny was too preoccupied to think about his wife's indiscretion. "A cop. The guy was a cop and I took his gun away," was all Johnny could say.

The words had barely passed his lips when the Braggs could hear sirens in the background. Gary, it seems, was a moonlighting policeman working days as a nonuniformed security guard at the store. He personally filed against Johnny a trumped-up charge of shoplifting and resisting arrest, to cover his own harassment of the former date whom he'd apparently not known was married.

Raymond Liggon once said, "Johnny Bragg and his wife were victims of circumstances. Some people resented the fact that Bragg, a Black man, was married to a White woman. That resentment sometimes triggered people's emotions into seeing what they wanted to see, because they felt threatened, rather than seeing what was really happening."

Once again Johnny Bragg, now fifty-one years old, was arrested. Despite Gail's testimony, the jury also saw what it wanted to see, and believed the White officer's tale of stolen beer. It didn't matter that Johnny was not a drinker and that he detested beer.

The judge found him guilty and sentenced him to sixty days in the county workhouse. He'd served only fifteen days before a parole violation warrant was issued and he was sent back to the dreaded Tennessee State Prison, where he stayed through the rest of April, May, June, and July 1977.

Gail visited Johnny several times, and each time he saw her, he worried that her physical condition seemed to keep deteriorating.

One seemingly uneventful evening two years earlier, Johnny, Gail, and Misti had been sitting down to dinner when Gail suddenly keeled over and blacked out. Johnny didn't think she was breathing. Near panic, he had screamed into the phone for paramedics, then left the receiver dangling while he gave her mouth-to-mouth resuscitation. Gail was rushed to the hospital, where it was diagnosed to be a worsening of a heart condition she had fought for several years.

Now in 1977, the last time Johnny saw Gail she had looked pale and weak. On July 21, two days after their last embrace, he received the news only that Gail had died of a blood clot to the brain—he was given no further details. Johnny was devastated. He had lost not only his love but also his best friend, and nobody would even bother to give him a proper explanation.

Johnny's sister, Dorothy, Gail's mother, several cousins and friends, along with Raymond Liggon and Sewell Jackson, attended thirty-eight-year-old Gail Green Bragg's funeral. She was interred at Woodlawn Cemetery, only a few hundred feet from Johnny's record company where she'd spent many a day helping him with his songs.

His six-year-old daughter, Misti, was put into a foster home.

On Wednesday, August 3, Johnny finally came before a parole board hearing. The board was astounded to find he had been confined for three and one-half months before the hearing was scheduled.

Appearing before them on Johnny's behalf were Raymond Liggon, Sewell Jackson, and the Reverends Dogan Williams and J. Richard Allison, along with Johnny's latest lawyer, Edward Sadler.

The parole board's spokesman uttered the words, "I think Johnny Bragg has suffered enough," and with that, Johnny's last day at the Tennessee State Prison ended. But his confinement didn't. He was sent back to the county workhouse to finish the remainder of his sixty-day sentence, but would be eligible in fifteen days to petition for suspension of the remaining sentence.

While in the county lockup, Johnny got word of yet another loss in his life. On August 16, just twenty-six days after Gail had passed away, Elvis Presley was discovered lying on the floor of his Graceland bathroom. Rushed to the Baptist Hospital in Memphis, he died at 3:30 P.M., of heart failure. Presley's funeral service at Graceland included 150 people inside and 75,000 more outside the gate. Johnny Bragg could not, of course, attend.

Back in January 1975, when Elvis had been hospitalized in Memphis with stomach problems, Johnny hadn't made time to visit him. "I was havin' a good time, pocket full of money and everythin', and I said I'd go see him later. But I didn't go up there. I cried a million times since then," Johnny recounts.

On August 22, 1977, Johnny finally left jail for the last time.

In 1981 Johnny Bragg used the legal system that had used him for so long. He and Robert Riley each sued Sun Records (no longer owned by Sam Phillips), charging that the company was a co-conspirator involved in selling both his and Riley's products overseas and avoiding royalty payments due them, by listing an H. Young as the writer of their solo and collaborative efforts recorded by the Prison-aires. Though Johnny sought five million dollars in damages and Riley three million, both settled out of court for only a few thousand dollars each.

As the South grew up to at least tolerate, if not accept, the notion of equality in the 1980s and 1990s, Johnny Bragg was no longer per-ceived as a threat or a symbol of change. He was just another old Black man who, over the previous twenty years, had managed to sur-vive within the system and finally make peace with his life.

He continued to perform through the '80s and '90s, including sing-ing at church services. He also became active in community affairs.

"Johnny helped a lot of people," says Don Hildebrand, the respected Nashville attorney who, though he never defended Bragg, has known the worst and best of Johnny since the 1970s.

"You might call it squandering his royalties, because for a long period of time he gave money away to people who were really in need. He also offered his services in support of the needy. There were even times that he paid mortgages for people. Once there was a Black Shriner Johnny kept out of the poorhouse for a time. There were other instances too. I remember a case when a sixteen-year-old girl was blown away by a police officer who shot her in the back three times. Johnny was there to comfort the family. He is totally loyal to his friends."

One of the things Johnny had regretted most was not being able to go to New York in 1956 for his BMI award. But in 1988 he got a second chance, when BMI held its annual Millionaires' Awards Banquet at the Vanderbilt Hotel in Nashville for those few elite writers whose songs had earned one million or more radio performances.

Since BMI's inception in 1940, over one million songs had been licensed but only 820 had reached the magic plateau. After thirty-five years of consistent radio play, "Just Walkin' in the Rain" joined that group and so, too, did John Henry Bragg.

BMI's president, Frances Preston, personally handed Johnny his plaque, with the comment, "This award is long overdue," as a standing ovation swept the hall.

His original Prisonaires partners had not been so fortunate. William Stewart died of a drug overdose in a rundown Florida motel in 1959. Marcel Sanders died in the late '60s. Ed Thurman was killed in an accident in 1973. And John Drue Jr. died of cancer in December 1977, in Lebanon, Tennessee.

On June 30, 1992, drawn by a news item he'd heard on the radio, Johnny stood outside his old penitentiary home watching a convoy of trucks, guards, and officials leave as the Tennessee State Prison doors swung closed for the last time.

Memories swept over him. The beatings, the mysterious deaths by "natural causes," the terrifying electric chair, the brutal guards, the attempts on his life . . .

Then and only then—as he realized that the old, inadequate facility was truly dead, while he was alive—could he appreciate that this was, after all, where he got his start as a singer, as a songwriter, as an entertainer, as a leader of a group, as a recording artist. He had found courage and freedom through the music he created here. He had found believers and friends in a governor and a warden here. And he found his maturity and his belief in God here.

Sam Phillips of Sun Records, the man who first recorded Johnny Bragg, Elvis Presley, Carl Perkins, Johnny Cash, Jerry Lee Lewis, and many others, says, "Music has succeeded where religion and politics failed."

In the story of Johnny Bragg we see music, religion, and politics so tightly tied together that one cannot see where one ends and the others begin.

Postscript

On June 8, 2000, Johnny Bragg, accompanied by his daughter, Misti, and longtime friend and lawyer Don Hildebrand, appeared in Memphis by invitation at a pre-screening of the A&E television special *Sam Phillips: The Man Who Invented Rock'n'Roll*. The documentary focusing on Phillips's life and his discoveries was to air on Father's Day, June 18.

Prior to production and at the request of the producers, I arranged to provide Johnny's services. With Hildebrand's help, the Tennessee State Penitentiary was opened—for the first time since *The Green Mile*, starring Tom Hanks, was shot there—in order for Johnny to do an interview and walking tour, including a visit to cell five on Walk Ten.

Standing on the ramp outside his former cell, Johnny sang a spontaneous a cappella rendition of "Just Walkin' in the Rain" and amazed all in attendance by doing the entire third verse in falsetto. About seven minutes of the footage shot that day was included in Sam's documentary.

Though seventy-five-year-old Johnny Bragg was a very minor celebrity in comparison to the legends appearing at the pre-screening and party, his onstage performance of "Just Walkin'" was acknowledged by many in attendance to be the sentimental highlight of the afternoon's events. When he finished with his trademark falsetto flourish, the response was a standing ovation led by Ike Turner, Jerry Lee Lewis, and Sam Phillips.

Contrary to Johnny's concern that his accomplishments might be forgotten as time passed, it is apparent that he is instead being well-remembered.

Discography

THE PRISONAIRES

JULY 8, 1953	A SIDE	*Just Walkin' in the Rain*	SUN 186
	B SIDE	*Baby Please*	
SEPT. 1, 1953	A SIDE	*My God Is Real*	SUN 189
	B SIDE	*Softly and Tenderly*	
NOV. 1, 1953	A SIDE	*A Prisoner's Prayer*	SUN 191
	B SIDE	*I Know*	
JULY 1, 1954	A SIDE	*There Is Love in You*	SUN 207
	B SIDE	*What'll You Do Next?*	
SEPT. 8, 1956	A SIDE	*Just Walkin' in the Rain*	SUN 186••
	B SIDE	*Baby Please*	

THE MARIGOLDS

APRIL 1955	A SIDE	*Rollin' Stone*	EXCELLO 2057
	B SIDE	*Why Don't You*	
JULY 1955	A SIDE	*Pork and Beans*	EXCELLO 2060•
	B SIDE	*Front Page Blues*	
JULY 1955	A SIDE	*Two Strangers*	EXCELLO 2061
	B SIDE	*Love You–Love You–Love You*	

JOHNNY BRAGG AND THE MARIGOLDS

MARCH 1956   A SIDE   *Beyond the Clouds*   EXCELLO 2078
            B SIDE   *Foolish Me!*

SEPT. 1956   A SIDE   *Juke Box Rock and Roll*   EXCELLO 2091
            B SIDE   *It's You Darling, It's You*

JOHNNY BRAGG

JUNE 1959   A SIDE   *True Love Will Never Die*   DECCA 30917
           B SIDE   *Just So That Someone Is Me*

SEPT. 1959   A SIDE   *Everything's Alright*   DECCA 30972
            B SIDE   *World of Make Believe*

SPRING 1969   A SIDE   *They're Talkin' About Me* ELBEJAY 001
             B SIDE   *Is It True?*

OCTOBER 1969   A SIDE   *I'm Free*   ELBEJAY 105
              B SIDE   *Hurt and Lonely*

1974   A SIDE   *They're Talkin' About Me*   INFERNO•••
      B SIDE   *Is It True?*

• The Solotones aka The Marigolds
•• Reissue
••• Rare British pressing

Notes

INTERVIEWS

Johnny Bragg	1996–2000
Misti Bragg	1997–2000
Larry Brinton	1998–1999
Senator Anna Belle Clement	1999–2000
Congressman Bob Clement	1999–2000
Judge Frank Clement Jr.	1999
Little Jimmy Dickens	1999
John Dougan	1999
Warden James Edwards	1998–2000
Galen Gart	1998
Marv Goldberg	1999
Bill Goodman	1999
Peter Grendysa	1997, 1999
Maxine Hanson	1999
Don Hildebrand	1996–2000
Tom Kittrell	1998
Eugenia Krump	1999
Colin Larkin	1999
George Lavatelli	1998–1999
Ann Locke	1998
Karina McDaniels	1999
Vince McGrath	1997
Andy McKaie	1998
Bill Millar	1998–1999
George Moonagian	1997, 1999

Jerry Osbourne	1998
Victor Pearlin	1999
Jerry Shilling	2000
Gordon Skadberg	1998–2000
Mary Smith	1998–1999
Gordon Stoker	1997, 1999
Ben Weisman	1997–1998

References

21–23 There was a throng . . . his eulogy.: *Tennessean* (6 November 1969)

27 Among Black children . . . high school diploma.: Don Doyle, *Nashville in the New South 1880–1930,* Knoxville, University of Tennessee Press (1985).

58 The story can't . . . uniquely his own.: Colin Escott, liner notes to "The Prisonaires" CD, Bear Family Records (1990).

67 I appreciate the confidence . . . in advance for them.: "Attorney to Succeed Swafford," *Nashville Banner* (10 January 1953).

68–69 Rumblings throughout the prison . . . not a rock was thrown.: "Warden Edwards Tightens Control on His Charges," *Nashville Banner* (18 March 1953).

70 Corporal punishment . . . came to an end.: Interview, James Edwards.

84 Sam Phillips was co-owner . . . first rock'n'roll record.: Martin Hawkins, liner notes to "Five Beats Behind Bars" LP, Charly Records; Colin Escott, *Good Rockin' Tonight,* St. Martin's Press (1992); Colin Escott, liner notes to "The Prisonaires" CD, Bear Family Records (1990).

84   The youngest . . . death of his father.: Peter Guralnick, *Last Train to Memphis: The Rise and Fall of Elvis Presley,* Little, Brown and Company (1994).

85   Clement was in favor of anything . . . good will outside the prison.: "Prison Singers May Find Fame With Record They Made in Memphis," *Memphis Commercial Appeal* (15 July 1953).

88–91   The Prisonaires arrived . . . shot at success.: The Prisonaires' first recording session is documented in an article by Clark Porteous in the *Memphis Commercial Appeal* (15 July 1953); in Colin Escott's *Good Rockin' Tonight;* in Bill Millar's "Johnny Bragg: Been Rainin' All My Life," *Melody Maker* (September 1973). Additional information from author's interviews.

91–92   Jud Phillips remembered . . . studio with Bragg.: "Johnny Bragg," *Nashville Banner* (29 September 1977); Peter Guralnick, *Last Train to Memphis: The Rise and Fall of Elvis Presley,* Little, Brown and Company (1994).

93   The Prisonaires represent . . . themselves.: "Prison Singers May Find Fame With Record They Made in Memphis," *Memphis Commercial Appeal* (15 July 1953).

94–95   Tennessee is renewing . . . civic club members.: "Warden Edwards Cites Prison Improvements," *Nashville Banner,* (17 June 1953).

99   . . . stars of the musical portion . . . Sun Records.: *Nashville Tennessean* (7 October 1953).

100   A Nashville Negro's vocal group . . . jobs at the prison.: "Prison Vocal Group Hits Jackpot Walkin' in the Rain," *Nashville Tennessean* (17 July 1953).

102   He wrote Sam . . . you do too.: Colin Escott, liner notes to "The Prisonaires" CD, Bear Family Records (1990).

104   It not only put the students . . . prisoners.: "N.Y. Warden Raps 'Liberty'; Prisonaires," *Jackson County Sentinel* (summer 1953).

104   No prisoner . . . alike here.: "N.Y. Warden Raps 'Liberty'; Prisonaires," *Jackson County Sentinel* (summer 1953).

112–13   The Prisonaires, a unique quintet . . . Pop, Hillbilly.: *Jet* (12 August 1953).

113   Sanders, who sang bass, was charged . . . where to start.: "Prisonaire Before Parole Board Wednesday," *Nashville Banner* (22 September 1953).

119   The Prisonaires have appeared . . . Governor Frank Clement.: "The Prisonaires, Unique Singing Group of Tennessee Prisoners," *Ebony* (November 1953).

121   Warden Edwards said . . . about $1.00.: "Prison Singers Left Unguarded," *Nashville Banner* (26 December 1953).

122   The Quartet . . . outside the prison.: "Visit Ban Excludes Prisonaires Quartet," *Nashville Tennessean* (12 February 1954).

129   . . . a liar . . . horse for a halter.: Various articles: *Nashville Banner* (25 May 1954, 17 June 1954, 18 June 1954, 28 June 1954, 18 July 1954).

136   Sam Phillips, who was thrifty . . . quartet's songs.: Colin Escott's liner notes, "The Prisonaires" CD, Bear Family Records (1990); also music historian Bill Millar.

136–37   It would take . . . "I Don't Want to Do It").: From interviews with George Moonagian, Peter Grendysa, Marv Goldberg, Bjorn Jentoff, George Lavatelli, Gordon Skadberg, and Bill Millar.

140   The governor officiated . . . admitted their guilt.: Interview with Warden Edwards.

140   Before one particular . . . talk to her.: Lee Seifert Greene, *Lead Me On*, Knoxville, University of Tennessee Press (1982).

150   During a speech by the former president . . . I am his.: "Truman Powerful in Party; Impressed by Governor Clement," Leslie T. Hart, *Nashville Banner* (25 April 1955).

150–51   Two days later . . . instant parole.: Charles L. Fontenay, *Nashville Banner* (27 April 1955).

152   It went on to lambaste the governor . . . for some fifty years.: "Songbird Out of a Cage," *Nashville Tennessean* (29 April 1955).

164–65   There were similarities . . . number three.: *Joel Whitburn's Top Pop Singles 1955–90*, Record Research Inc./Billboard

(1997); Steve Knopper, *Music Hound Lounge Music, The Essential Album Guide to Martini Music and Easy Listening,* Visible Ink (1998); Donald Clark, *Penguin Encyclopedia of Popular Music,* Penguin (1989).

165   As of the 1990s, . . . singles worldwide.: Fred Bronson, *Billboard's Hottest Hot 100 Hits,* Billboard (1991).

168   It was not his best . . . better speech.: Steve Jacks, *Anna Belle Clement O'Brien, The First Lady of Tennessee Politics,* Morgan County Publishing Company (1995).

169   Though his speech . . . political Billy Graham.: *Newsweek* (13 August 1956).

173   On one song . . . clapped their hands: Craig Morrison, *Go Cat Go: Rockabilly Music and Its Makers,* Urbana, University of Illinois Press (1996).

182   A 1959 news account . . . for his life.: "Song Writer Could Be Marked Man In Prison," Jack Setters, *Nashville Banner* (20 November 1959).

185   I fully believe Johnny is completely rehabilitated: "Hit Songwriter May Quit Prison," *Nashville Tennessean* (17 January 1959).

187–88   Bomar and parole board both cited in *Nashville Banner* (28 January 1959).

188   I'll always have witnesses . . . behind bars again.: "Song Writer Bids Adieu To Prison," *Nashville Banner* (28 January 1959).

189   A year in prison . . . college.: "Year In Prison Worth 4 At College: Bragg," Jim Scott, *Nashville Banner* (29 January 1959).

196   Johnny Bragg, who rocketed . . . several morals cases.: "Walkin' in Rain Composer Jailed," Mickey McLinden, *Nashville Banner* (18 January 1960).

197   What does Johnny Bragg . . . the truth. I've nothing to worry about.: "Been Living Right, Composer Insists," Mickey McLinden, *Nashville Banner* (20 January 1960).

197   Davidson County grand jury . . . violated parole.: "Negro Singer is Indicted," Associated Press (23 January 1960).

198   The State Pardons and . . . against him.: "Negro Songwriter Called Delinquent," United Press International (24 January 1960).

198   Bragg had testified . . . fifty-five years.: "Bragg Case Goes to Jury Today," *Nashville Banner* (25 January 1960).

204–05   With Elvis around . . . it's going to be.: "Presley to Visit Assembly," Ken Morrell, *Nashville Banner* (6 March 1961); Red O'Donnell, "Elvis Does Free Shot for Assembly," *Nashville Banner* (8 March 1961). See also: *Memphis Commercial Appeal* (9 March 1961).

Index

About the Author

Jay Warner was raised in Brooklyn, New York. While still in his teens he took on the subject of music history, writing his first work, *The History of Rock & Roll*, 1954–1963 (Crystal Publications).

By 1973 Jay had convinced the Wes Farrell Organization to hire him. He started as a professional song plugger, and three and a half years later was moved to Los Angeles as vice president of Farrell's publishing empire.

In 1977, on a dare, Jay wrote the definitive text on song writing and music publishing, *How to Have Your Hit Song Published* (Hal Leonard Publications). It was the first in-depth volume ever written dealing entirely with the publishing, copyright, and songwriting industry. The bestseller has been in print for twenty-three years and is in its fifth edition. That same year he became vice president at The Entertainment Company (the forerunner of SBK EMI) and began by organizing and running their West Coast base.

During 1979 Jay was elected to the ASCAP advisory board. He also recieved the American Song Festival's "Ears of the Year" award and in 1980 won the award again for an unprecedented second time.

In 1980 he founded and became president of the Creative Music Group, the worldwide publishing arm of the K-Tel International organization. He established a network of publishing operations in twenty-two countries, a first for independent publishers. He also developed one of the first internal divisions in America devoted to full-time pursuit of music coordination of films and music administration.

In 1983 Jay formed his own company, The Jay Warner Music Group. Within a year and a half of its establishment, Jay's company racked up fourteen hit singles and seven chart albums. His company was named the number-two independent publisher of 1983 by *Billboard* magazine.

In mid-1984 Warner merged his company with The Music Group and became president of the combined publishing organizations, where he successfully oversees the company's operations to this day.

As a publisher, Jay has worked with many diverse catalogues and writers, including Barry Manilow, Bruce Springsteen, Rick James, Jimmy Webb, Carol Sager, the Rascals, Bob Gaudio (Four Seasons), REO Speedwagon, the Commodores, the Emotions, Steppenwolf, Lakeside, Ben Weisman (writer of fifty-seven Elvis Presley songs), and many others. He has published songs recorded by artists ranging from Elvis and Streisand to Springsteen and Whitney Houston.

In 1993 the six-time Grammy winner with over 120 Top 40 hits to his credit had his epic musical mosaic published, *The Billboard Book of American Singing Groups* (Watson-Guptil), a first-ever history of vocal groups from the 1940s through 1990. During 1996 Jay was elected to the board of the Vocal Group Hall of Fame and hosted their inaugural induction ceremony in October 1998. In 1997 Jay wrote another bestseller, *Billboard's American Rock & Roll in Review* (Schirmer/Simon & Schuster), endorsed by thirty-seven major stars from Neil Diamond to the Beach Boys.

Never placing his publishing hat far from his writing tools, Jay finished out the last year of the millennium with two platinum ("TLC" and "Silk the Shocker") and two gold ("Total" and the soundtrack from *Blue Streak*) albums, as well as a hit single by Mariah Carey, "Heartbreaker/If You Should Ever Be Lonely."

Jay and his wife, Jackie, reside in Los Angeles along with their beloved cairn terrier, Napoleon.

If you like the book, you'll love the music!

The Prisonaires/Marigolds/Solotones/Johnny Bragg anthology includes:

That Chick's Too Young to Fry	Prisonaires	Sun
Just Walkin' in the Rain	Prisonaires	Sun
Baby Please	Prisonaires	Sun
Softly and Tenderly	Prisonaires	Sun
A Prisoner's Prayer	Prisonaires	Sun
No More Tears	Prisonaires	Sun
What'll You Do Next?	Prisonaires	Sun
There Is Love in You	Prisonaires	Sun
What About Frank Clement, a Mighty, Mighty Man	Prisonaires	Sun
Friends Call Me a Fool	Prisonaires	Sun
Lucille, I Want You	Prisonaires	Sun
Surleen	Prisonaires	Sun
All Alone and Lonely	Prisonaires	Sun
Rockin' Horse	Prisonaires	Sun
Rollin' Stone	Marigolds	Excello
Pork and Beans	Solotones (Marigolds)	Excello
Love You–Love You–Love You	Marigolds	Excello
Juke Box Rock and Roll	Marigolds	Excello
True Love Will Never Die	Johnny Bragg & The Jordanaires	Decca
They're Talkin' About Me	Johnny Bragg	ElBeJay
Is It True?	Johnny Bragg	ElBeJay
Hurt and Lonely	Johnny Bragg	ElBeJay